THE OUTDOOR EYE:
A Sportsman's Guide

AN OUTDOOR LIFE BOOK

THE OUTDOOR EYE:
A Sportsman's Guide

How to see, hear, interpret
the signs of wilderness and wildlife

Charles Elliott

Illustrated by
Tom Beecham

OUTDOOR LIFE • FUNK & WAGNALLS
New York

To RWW
An outdoor partner
who dedicates himself to others

CONTENTS

Introduction

MANY OF US go through life without ever really seeing the greatest show on earth. So preoccupied are we with artificial things, that we take time only for superficial glimpses at the scenes which change subtly from season to season, and the actors which come and go. We miss most of the main show, with its humor and pathos, its comedy and high drama, its tenderness and courage and stark terror.

The stage for our show is the swamps and mountains and seashore, the desert and woodland of all outdoors, and its cast of characters the creatures which inhabit the wild spaces of the earth.

For one who is fully aware of what is happening in every part of the outdoors, nature's perennial show is fascinating to observe. That awareness comes generally through the mediums of sight, sound and smell, and occasionally through touch.

America is moving outdoors. Each year a growing army of men, women and their families discover the pleasures of camping, hiking, hunting, boating, fishing and skiing. Every year the study of birds, flowers, butterflies, trees and rocks gains new disciples.

Many of these people are, in a sense, newcomers to the outdoor scene. All their lives they literally have been imprisoned in the heart of urban areas. They live amidst crowded buildings, breathe carbon monoxide, and hear only the din of city streets. Their senses have been dulled by the routine of urban existence.

Then one day, by design or accident, they suddenly escape into a land beyond the city limits and find a whole new world, filled with the smell of fresh air, the music of wind and running water, the beauty of clouds and waterfalls and massive mountain ranges that reach to the tall skyline. They discover the vast pleasure of identifying some bird or flower new to them, or of seeing a deer bound into the woods, or a cardinal or tanager slip furtively to its nest hidden in a tangle of foliage. And yet, because they do not know where, when or how to look and listen, they miss many interesting and dramatic sights of the field, swamp and forest.

Not everyone has a good outdoor eye, ear or other sense. Excellence in this department may be acquired in only two ways—experience or training. It comes naturally—through experience—to a boy raised on a farm, or to a man who has spent his life in the forest. Because he has observed them from the time he was old enough to toddle, every movement, every sound, every mark in the soft dirt of the earth tells him a story, gives him a picture of what is going on around him. Often in country occupied by potentially dangerous animals, his correct interpretation of those sights and sounds may mean the difference between life and death.

I once hunted the southwest Texas semidesert country along the Rio Grande. The place was loaded with outsized diamondback rattlesnakes, and when we moved afoot from one spot to another it was prudent to exercise extreme caution.

Early one morning I was on the trail of a big-footed buck, and since a number of record heads had been taken from this region, I could visualize a trophy rack on our den wall at home. The tracks were so fresh that I expected momentarily to either see the buck ahead or jump him out of a thicket, and in the excitement lost a measure of precaution.

One of several things could have stopped me from stepping over a small bush in the deer trail. A slight movement on the other side may have caught my eye. I may have smelled a faint musky odor or, in the stillness, heard the rasp of sand grains moved by a heavy body. It could have been reflex. More plausibly, it was the tracks of the buck, where the animal had paused in the trail, performed a bit of a jig step, then leaped far over the bush instead of merely stepping over it.

I was struck by the fact that this had not been the normal pattern of the deer's tracks, and I stopped to try to reason it out. Either the buck had seen me and spooked, or something else had startled it. I decided not to take a chance. I gave that bush a wide berth, walking on open ground around it, and by the time I arrived at the other side was almost sure of what I'd find.

The largest rattlesnake I ever met was coiled there, with its head high enough off the ground to hit me above my boot tops. A less experienced hunter, in the excitement of pursuit, could have stepped squarely into range of those lethal fangs.

There is an old saying that out of every three persons who pass through a stretch of country, one will see nothing, one will observe only the things that interest him—whether it be birds, animal tracks, mushrooms or what—and the third will miss very few of the sights and sounds. In these modern times, the percentage of persons who miss the most will be at least ten times as high as those who use all their senses as they travel through strange or wild country.

There was a time when those percentages ran the other way. The early outdoorsman in this country who failed to read the signs and heed the sights and sounds was gambling with his scalp. To those early American outdoorsmen—red and white alike—a crushed blade of grass, an upturned pebble, a bent twig, a stick or green leaf floating on a stream all carried a message. When the white man first brought guns into the back country, his presence was betrayed by the inch-square patches used to seat a rifle ball in his muzzle-loader. Sharp-eyed Indians found them in the woods.

Because of the extreme keenness of the red hunter and warrior, our pioneering forefathers had to remain constantly alert. It was necessary to see and instantly identify every sound and movement in the woods and on the plains. Failing to read just one correctly might be the last mistake they ever made.

Without the necessity of having to kill wild game to feed our families, or of protecting them from unfriendly Indians or renegades, being alert to everything that goes on about us in the American outdoors loses its importance. So most of us never make the effort, and thereby miss many delightful hours beyond the realm of walls, doors and windows. Our enjoyment of the wild places may take in the splendor of mountains, pastel sunsets, the kaleidoscope of autumn, the fury of a storm, but seldom goes deeper. As hikers and nature lovers, we miss most of the little dramas which occupy the outdoor stage. As hunters and fishermen, we fail to observe and understand sights and sounds which might bring us success instead of failure.

Someone once said that if you wrote down everything that goes on in the course of a day under one large tree, you could write a book about it. That may be true, but only within the scope of your awareness, experience and knowledge.

The purpose of this book is to point out certain lessons, drawn from my own experience and the experience of others, which may increase both your hunting and fishing success and your overall enjoyment of the outdoors.

1 Do You Have a Good Game Eye?

I THOUGHT I had one of the best game eyes until I began to meet some real woodsmen in the far corners of the earth. One of my first lessons was from Paul Germain.

Paul and I were sitting on a hillside in the distant reaches of the Yukon Territory. Below us lay a valley with scattered clumps of timber. Beyond the valley, a tremendous mountain thrust its treeless crest against the sky.

Paul was my Indian guide. Only that morning we had started a month-long hunt, on which we hoped to find a white ram with the biggest, widest curl in that land close to the Arctic Circle. Paul pointed to a distant peak.

"Sheep," he said.

I swept the jagged skyline with my 8X binoculars and finally located a microscopic white dot. I studied it for half a minute and shook my head.

"Nertz, Paul. You don't see nothing but a white rock."

"O.K.," he said, nodding agreeably.

I turned my binoculars to another slope to look for signs of life and the guide touched my arm.

"Sheep," he insisted.

Again I swung my glasses to the "rock" and found that it had moved. With his unaided vision, Paul had identified a Dall ram that with 8-power glasses I had seen as a piece of white quartz.

Until that moment, I had thought my ability to see game was equal to any woodsman's. But long before the end of my month on the slopes which drain into the Arctic Ocean, I had to concede that what I considered my good game eye was only moderately perceptive vision.

Paul was eternally pointing out such creatures as the ptarmigan, its mottled coat in the process of changing from its brown summer dress to all white, the mixed feathers blending so perfectly with the rocks and lichens and reindeer moss that it was all but invisible from a few feet away.

Once we jumped a big grizzly out of a thicket along the creek. It was dark brown with a golden saddle across its shoulders—a color phase I wanted more than any other as a trophy. With my eyes glued on the bear, I threw the rifle to my shoulder, but Paul said quietly, "Cub following behind."

Not until then did I see the ball of fur, hardly visible in the high brush. Without the guide's sharp eye, I might have unknowingly violated one of the cardinal principles of sportsmanship, and bagged a female with young.

Before the month was out, I had given a lot of thought to the qualities that make for a good game eye, and to analyzing why my guide's vision appeared to be so much better than mine. I was sure there was not that much difference between our eyes.

We all know what we see, but not one person in a thousand can explain *how* he sees it, or the processes the eye goes through to flash an image to the brain.

HOW THE EYE FUNCTIONS

The human eye is a remarkable organ, composed of twenty-seven operating units. Though much more complicated, it functions on the same principle as a simple camera. Rays of light come into the eye through the cornea, where

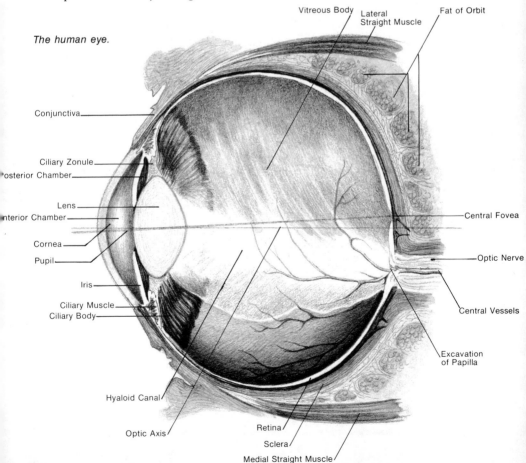

The human eye.

they are refracted and broken up into different wave lengths. The lens of the eye, behind the cornea, refracts the light still further, and it is distributed to the interior of the eye according to the laws of geometrical optics.

The screen of the eye is the retina. The picture we see is formed there, minute in size and inverted, exactly like that which comes through the lens of the camera.

The retina is composed of millions of tiny nerves called cones and rods. The cones pick up the light of varying wave lengths, which we see as color. People with cones which do not work properly, and certain animals whose retinas lack cones, are color-blind.

One theory says there are three types of cones, each of which responds to all colors. But one is especially sensitive to red, another to blue and a third to green, which are the basic colors from which the combinations that form all colors are derived.

The sensitivity of the cones gradually decreases as the light dims, and the more than one hundred million rods take over, so that we can see varying degrees of brightness, but the hues fade.

The picture we see is transmitted through the optic nerve to the brain. If it is a fuzzy picture, the brain instantly signals back to the lens, which changes its shape and power of refraction and brings what we are observing into focus. This is so automatic that we never think about it at all, but when we change our vision from an object inches or feet from the eye, to another a hundred yards or a mile away, the focus of the lens changes to give us a clear picture.

The construction of the eye in all creatures apparently is based on the same general principle, but since we are unable to communicate by words with them, we have no way of positively comparing our vision with theirs. By certain experiments we have been able to determine that differences do exist between human eyes and those of other animals.

Some of the cats, for example, have elliptical eye pupils, so that in bright daylight the pupil appears as a narrow vertical slit that lets in a limited amount of light. This type of cat is to a large extent a night hunter, and nature has so arranged its vision that as the amount of daylight decreases, the slit expands until it may be fully rounded and the cat can see where the eyes of man would be blacked out completely.

Other creatures, like the mountain sheep and antelope, are equipped with eyesight which some naturalists think is comparable to man's vision through 7X or 8X binoculars. This long-distance perception is a necessary safety factor on the big, open range where they make their homes.

Once, when I was hunting antelope with Max Wilde, a hunting partner of Buffalo Bill Cody and later a famous western guide and outfitter on his own, I located a buck antelope through my field glasses. The animal was so far away that I had not seen it with my naked eye, yet the buck had its head up and was staring directly at us. When I remarked on this, the old guide chuckled.

"By the time you spotted him, he had already counted the buttons on your jacket and knew what caliber gun you are shooting."

SEEING COLOR

When I was told that members of the deer family are mostly color-blind, I did not believe it and argued the point at great length with some of my biologist friends.

"It is movement they see and not how you are dressed," the technical people assured me.

"Just put on a bright yellow coat," I said, "and sit on a deer stand. Not a buck or doe will come within half a mile of you."

I later learned that in a sense we were both right. Colors such as white, blue or bright yellow have a wavelength of such proportions that they usually are in strong contrast to the more subdued hues around them and stand out to any eye. Yet, even though an animal may be able to spot them in relation to the intensity of light they reflect, it is the movement which more quickly puts it to flight. It also appears that the less-bright reds and yellows do blend in such a way that a color-blind eye does not pick them up, even though they may be highly visible to color-conscious eyesight.

Jim Gay, a friend and guide, and I were hunting elk in the Shirley Mountains of central Wyoming. Fresh elk and deer tracks were everywhere, but we did not seem to be able to contact any of the critters in person.

I proposed to Jim that he stand in the edge of a small clearing at the mouth of a canyon, while I made a big circle in an effort to drive the big bull whose tracks we had been following out of the gulch and through the clearing.

Jim wore a vivid red coat, so I suggested that he conceal himself well to break up his obvious outline. He paid me not the slightest attention, but while I made my drive, took his stand in an open spot in the bright sunlight.

I did not know this until I had almost completed my circle. I never did catch up with the elk, but jumped several mule deer in the canyon. They slipped out ahead of me, staying just far enough in front so that when I got close enough to see my crimson-clad partner, shining like a neon sign in the edge of the clearing, the deer were just passing him, less than thirty feet away. I stopped and watched, and while their actions indicated that they were well aware of my presence, apparently they did not see Jim.

Since then I have done a bit of experimenting of my own with hunting clothes of various hues, and am reasonably well convinced that movement and scent will give a deer hunter away much more quickly than color, though I am sure they are more aware of the highly intensive type.

Dressed for turkey hunting, I have crouched motionless in a blind and had whitetail deer practically step on me. When one is out to call up a gobbler, he had best leave those loud colors in the bottom of his dresser drawer.

"In a turkey blind," one of my swamper friends said, "even a pair of blood-shot eyes is too much color."

I dress in the conventional jungle camouflage suit, splotched with blends of greens, browns and dull yellows. I also put on camouflage gloves and wear a mask over my face. I have made photographs of hunting partners dressed in such an outfit and concealed in a clump of foliage, and you have to look hard at it to find anything that resembles a man.

I sat without batting an eyelid while he browsed on leaves no more than inches from my face.

Last spring I was garbed like this and perched on a slope in my favorite mountain woods. With plaintive yelps I was teasing an amorous gobbler on the hill across a narrow cove, and he was making the forest ring with his demands that I come across and share his affections. A stealthy footstep to my right caused me to shift my eyes. A small buck deer was grazing toward me. I sat without batting an eyelid while he browsed on leaves no more than inches from my face, and walked on past, so close I could have put my fingers into his ribs.

When he reached the windward side and caught my scent, it was a different story. Whatever the perfume I exuded, it sure hit him wrong. He turned a near flip, ran into a tree and took off on such a long bound downhill that I thought he was going to fly. The wise old gobbler, convinced that all was not exactly hunky-dory in the woodpile, suddenly remembered the little hen waiting for him in the next county.

I compared this experience with one the fall before when, dressed in blaze-orange, I sat on a stand over a well-used deer trail and watched a buck approach within a hundred yards before he saw me. I had not moved, but the contrast in brightness between my jacket and the background must have caught his eye. Since I remained still, he did not spook, but simply walked around me at what he considered a safe distance. For half a dozen minutes he was well within range, but I passed him up because he was too small.

I am not recommending against blaze-orange or any other bright color.

Many states now require that a deer hunter wear reds or yellows for protection, and generally this regulation has been responsible for a marked decrease in the number of hunting accidents and deaths.

What I am saying is that within my experience, while the color-blind eye may not pick up the bright hues as quickly as an eye which contains the proper cones, the light reflection from those vivid colors does make them more visible to any eye. And hunters outfitted in color continue to bag deer, while safeguarding their own skins.

NIGHT VISION

One of the great differences between human and other animal eyes is the amount of visual purple, or rhodopsin, the eye contains. This is a chemical in the retina which makes it sensitive to subdued light. While we as humans are far inferior to most animals in the ability to see at night, some humans are blessed with more rhodopsin than others. I must admit that I am one of the underprivileged whose eyes practically go out when the sun goes down. Good vision in poor light is a great help to any hunter.

Anson Eddy, my hunting companion and guide for many years in Wyoming's Thorofare country, could see at night almost as well as I could see in the daytime. Anson had spent all his years in the back country. During the winters he trapped in isolated mountain valleys he could reach only on snowshoes, sometimes with a partner, more often alone. With the temperature far below zero for weeks at a time, with blizzards and whiteouts and avalanches as his frequent companions on the trail, he had to stay alert to survive. In the fall he worked as a guide with a local hunting outfitter, and during most of the remaining months he served with the U.S. Forest Service or scouted the high country on his own.

Anson and I were riding down a trail along the edge of a meadow one night. We had hunted until dark and were on our way back to camp by starlight, which gives an amazing amount of illumination on a clear night at high altitudes. He turned in his saddle.

"Look at that old bull standing up there in the meadow."

I rode a few feet to the rear and couldn't see much farther than the hind end of Anson's horse, but I pretended that I could see the animal he had pointed out.

"Oh yeah," I said. "Sure. How about that?"

We rode on for at least thirty seconds before I glimpsed a movement just off the trail. By straining my eyes, I made out the black silhouette of an animal.

"Look," I said, "there's a moose."

"Uh-huh," Anson grunted. "That's the one I was telling you about."

The experts say that the ability to see at night may be inherited, but that it can be acquired if no physical defects are involved. Vitamin A is the substance that helps to build the supply of visual purple in the rods of the retina. A vitamin-A deficiency reduces the sensitivity of the eye to light.

The ancient Egyptians probably never heard of vitamin A or rhodopsin, but to improve their vision in the darkness, they ate large quantities of liver, which we know today is loaded with vitamin A.

I have a friend who trained for night duty in World War II by living in a dark room for weeks at a time. He was also dosed with vitamin A to build up his supply of rhodopsin. He never saw daylight on his entire tour of duty. When he got home, he said he could have taken up burglary with a fair amount of success.

Staying out of bright lights over a long period might help a hunter see better in the late and early hours of the day, but few of us will go to such extremes.

I am sure that the best my night vision has ever been was during that fall and winter years ago when I served with a crew of mountain boys, constructing trails in a remote section of Georgia's Blue Ridge. We lived in a rough building left by an old logging camp, with cracks wide enough to throw a cat through—or at least a kitten—so the mountaineers brought their hound dogs from home to help us endure the cold and dispose of our table scraps.

There was one more reason for the acquisition of our hounds. The region through which our trails ran was loaded with the tracks of bobcats, foxes, raccoons and opossums, and all of us were hungry for a bit of canine midnight music.

We had planned to make a couple of hunts a week, but almost before we knew it, the coon and bobcat chasing had developed into a nightly affair. When we came in from a day's work, we would sleep for a couple of hours, then cook and eat and call the dogs.

They were not especially particular hounds and would run anything that left tracks on the ground, and when some creature went into the base of a hollow tree or under a rock cliff, it was anybody's guess as to what we would find there. Like the night we tried to catch the skunk and it caught us first—but that is another story.

We'd get back to camp before daylight, sleep two more hours, eat breakfast and go to work on the trail system until time to come by camp and start hunting again.

We hunted in the darkness, without a flashlight or lantern and when the dogs treed, we would build a fire—as much for warmth as for light, for on some of those winter nights the bottom dropped out of the thermometer.

In those days I did not know what a vitamin was, and do not remember eating any liver, but the night after night of running up and down those pitch-black mountainsides must have built up an excessive amount of visual purple, even though I was using my eyes as much in the daylight as in the darkness.

Many night hunters I know have exceptionally good eyes in the dark, possibly developed over many seasons of running with their hounds through the night. This surely must be one method of helping to build the supply of rhodopsin, and one of the most delightful if you are a hound-dog man. Being able to see in dim light is one of the assets that goes with a good game eye.

2 The Hunter's Eye

SUPPOSE WE assume that any healthy human eye is constructed and operates like any other healthy human eye. This suggests that your eyes and mine are fundamentally as sound as those of the best guides and woodsmen to be found anywhere. We can see as far as they do, our eyes can focus as quickly as theirs, and at least some of us are blessed with a substantial amount of visual purple.

What then, we may wonder, might be the difference between their competence and ours in finding game and seeing other creatures that our eyes seem to miss?

In looking back across many years of association with dozens of guides and outdoorsmen from the arctic to the tropics, I can come to only one conclusion: the relative proficiency of an outdoor eye is its capacity to *interpret* what it sees.

The ability to see every movement and every sign and understand its meaning came as naturally to my old hunting partner Anson Eddy as drawing breath. His game eye was superb, but I never knew how quick and sure it really was until one afternoon when we were climbing a well-worn game trail through a stretch of heavy timber late in the day.

The earth was damp and our steps were silent as we slipped along upwind, a few yards at a time, pausing often for a minute or more to look and listen. We both preferred this type of hunting to clattering along on horseback.

We paused momentarily where the trail cut through a thick stand of trees. I have no idea how much I was concentrating on the timber ahead or whether I was concentrating at all, but I was suddenly startled by the crash of brush downhill to our right.

Anson was carrying his rifle on its sling over his shoulder, but in an instant the rifle was in his hands and pointed toward the crashing. He had made his move with the speed of a quick-draw handgun artist. By the time I first saw the elk, Anson had aimed his rifle and passed up a shot at a fair-size bull which apparently had been bedded down in the timber.

11

I had seen the animal when it moved, but my only reaction was curiosity. I did not even think about my rifle until several long bounds had put the bull out of sight. Anson spotted the elk the instant it moved, and his experience told him what the animal was and that the bull wasn't good enough. My partner's reaction had put him in position to take the elk while I stood there with my mouth open and my rifle slung over my shoulder.

Once I missed a big turkey gobbler because I did not know what I was seeing. I had hunted all of one morning during the spring season without hearing a bird. Almost always, the toms stop gobbling about eight or ten o'clock, but they often cluck or yelp out of curiosity at any time of day. Many veteran turkey hunters spend the entire day in a blind, calling now and then to attract any gobbler that comes by or feeds within sound of a yelper.

I stuck out the morning in a blind. After a sandwich at noon, I grew restless. Parts of my anatomy ached from long contact with the ground, and the flies

The gobbler flattened himself in the depression and crept up the hill.

were bothering me. So I decided to wander and look for fresh scratching and other sign to indicate where I would find a gobbler the following morning.

Since I was in no hurry, I moved slowly, cutting across the high, flat coves, stopping on the backbones of the ridges to sit awhile and work my yelper. On one high ridge, I found a cool breeze and an old log in the shadow of a clump of pines. I sat down, yelped a few notes with my cedar box, and then put it into my pocket. The spot was so pleasant that I sat there for half an hour before the log began to develop knots I hadn't noticed before.

I got up, stretched, and went slowly downhill through a laurel thicket. When I reached a narrow cove, the corner of my eye caught a movement close to a decaying treetop that lay in the bottom of the cove below me, not more than seventy-five feet away.

The forest floor was otherwise so clean that I was sure I could see anything that moved across it. My first thought was that I had scared up a raccoon or wildcat, but I wasn't sure.

I stood still, watched a few minutes, saw nothing, and walked slowly downhill with my gun ready. As I approached the treetop, wings roared on the hill above me to my left. I swung around in time to see a big gobbler pitch over the crest of the ridge and disappear. He was gone before I could get my gun up.

I could not believe what I had seen until I went over the ground thoroughly. As every turkey hunter knows, a gobbler that stands four feet tall can duck behind a bush that seems no larger than a church fan and disappear as though the earth had swallowed him. But the ground around the treetop was free of small bushes.

A long depression no more than twelve inches deep ran down from the ridge to the treetop. The gobbler had flattened himself in it and had slipped up the hill. When I reached a point where I would have seen the bird if I hadn't been watching the treetop so carefully, the gobbler flew over the crest.

If only I had sprinted downhill on first glimpsing movement, the gobbler would have flushed and I would have been close enough to kill it on the wing. My eyesight had been good enough, but my experience didn't tell me what that movement meant.

One thing that experience teaches a hunter, fisherman, bird student, hiker or wildlife photographer is where and how to look for outdoor creatures.

MOVING AND MOTIONLESS GAME

A moving animal is, of course, much more easily spotted than one lying down or standing motionless in the forest. Yet seldom is any creature that is awake and unalarmed motionless for very long. Even relaxed, most of them are constantly on the alert. They betray their presence in many ways—the turn of a head, the flick of an ear or tail, the batting of an eye.

One of my friends, a well-known ornithologist, has an excellent game eye. As far as I know, he has never carried a gun in the woods, but no creature

Animals betray their presence in many ways—the turn of a head, the flick of an ear or tail, the batting of an eye.

moves within the limit of his vision without being seen. I was with him when he spotted a woodcock on its nest, fifty feet away. The bird was so perfectly camouflaged that although my friend pointed out the exact spot, I couldn't see the woodcock until we were within ten feet of it. How did he do it? He had seen the bird close and then open one eye.

The ornithologist also pointed out deer, raccoons, squirrels and a variety of wild inhabitants that I would never have spotted on my own, even though I am sure I see as much as the average hunter. There is no explanation for his skill except half a century of studying birds with and without field glasses.

My guess is that you don't have to chase around after birds for fifty years to improve your game eye. The hours you spend in the fields and woods, conscientiously training yourself to understand what you see, add up fast.

Jack Crockford, who has had more experience with whitetail deer than any of my other outdoor partners, says that most tyro hunters expect to see a whole deer and do not spend enough time looking for a motionless hoof, ear or part of an antler or for a patch of white on muzzle, throat or tail that is all but hidden by a screen of trees or brush. The trick, of course, is knowing that these things look out of place in the thick growth.

On one of our mule-deer hunts in Wyoming, Jim Gay pointed out something about spotting motionless game that had never occurred to me before. Jim is a noted taxidermist and guide who lives in Laramie.

"Almost every object in the timber or a thicket," he told me, "is vertical, so one of the things to look for is a horizontal line or object. Very often it is the back of a deer or elk that's standing still."

"You must see a lot of logs and flat-topped rocks," I remarked.

"Sure I do," Jim admitted, "but I also see plenty of game that I would otherwise miss."

Although hunters look for a whole deer, often they see only a part of the animal.

KNOWING WHERE TO LOOK

Jim agreed that where to look is just as important as how. You expect to see elk on the meadows and in the highland parks early in the morning and during twilight. In the middle of the day they often bed down or stand in the shade of the trees, asleep or at least relaxed on their feet. Early in the season before winter sets in, elk may be on the highest mesas or ridges. Cold winds and deep snow drive them down to lower country.

I can verify that with emphasis. One of the most amazing hunts I ever had in the Thorofare was during the last two weeks of October. Winter was early that year and when we packed into the country, the other hunting camps had moved out. Snow was a foot deep on the level and drifting over the trails and banks and in the high passes. Blizzard velocity winds howled across the high meadows around and above timberline. Earlier in the season, one usually finds the elk in these alpine parks, but weather conditions being what they were, it seemed that every elk in northwestern Wyoming had moved into the timbered pockets and canyons along Thorofare Creek. Never have I seen such a concentration of wild bulls and cows. Fresh sign was everywhere and it was not uncommon to have a herd of the animals explode like a covey of quail out of a small thicket. We looked over a lot of bulls before we finally took our trophies.

Almost every object in the timber is vertical, so look for objects or lines that are horizontal.

17

Over the twenty-five years or more that I hunted the Thorofare and the headwater country of the Yellowstone River, I learned that the feeding and resting places of the elk depended largely on the weather—and in later years on the hunting pressure—and we never had too much trouble locating a good bull.

Jim Gay expressed this thought very well about mule-deer bucks when he said, "Until a hunter knows where to look, he wastes plenty of time watching places the deer won't be. A buck seldom walks through the middle of a clearing. Instead he travels just inside the line of trees. If there is an open slope topped by rimrock, chances are that you'll find an old buck lying out of the wind in the sunshine at the base of the rimrock during the middle of the day.

"A storm," he went on, "usually puts a deer herd in the timber or on the lee side of a hill. All game animals have habits involving protection, comfort, and food, and you have to know enough about each species so that you'll know where to look."

The same holds true for most wild creatures. The conditions which determine where you might see them include weather, preference of terrain, abundance of feed, mating and other habits, migration, and hunting pressure if they are one of the game species.

As an extreme example, you would not expect to find a colony of beavers in the middle of a desert, with water hundreds of miles away, or penguins along the Amazon.

On the other hand we know that quail and pheasants feed and live on the ground, and that we are likely to find ducks on or reasonably adjacent to water. Boiling it down to a finer point, we know that the ground-using birds choose certain kinds of habitat and that the species of ducks you see will largely depend on the type of aquatic surroundings and the conditions which make them highly habitable at the moment.

A storm usually puts a deer herd in the timber or on the lee side of a hill.

Having a quick, knowledgeable game eye is very important in wing shooting. Pheasants, quail, doves and waterfowl each have a distinct pattern of flight, and a gunner versed in the antics of a given species knows where and how to look and reacts quickly.

Once I went with a friend on his first hunt for bobwhites. He was an expert duck hunter and could spot a weaving line of waterfowl long before I saw it. I often accused him of operating with built-in radar.

On our first covey of quail, the dogs pointed and we walked in behind them, looking straight ahead for the rise. The explosion of birds was to my friend's right and slightly to his rear. Two of the quail cut around behind us, and when they were out of the danger zone, I downed one that was flying through the pines. My partner swung on his heel when the birds roared off the ground, but they were gone before he could mark them and decide on a bird. It is my guess that his inexperience did not allow him to put his eye in the right place soon enough. Before the day was over, however, he got the hang of quail shooting and was killing birds with the precision and accuracy of an old-timer.

Timber shooting for mallards requires a sharp game eye. You hear the whisper of their wings and the birds talking overhead, but you don't dare show your face by looking up if you want a shot. Many times you can't shoot until the spaces in the treetops are filled with drakes and hens hurtling toward the stool. If you know where to look when the time comes to shoot, you spot them soon enough to fold one or two before they react to your movement or some other sign of danger and flare away.

IDENTIFYING GAME

Nowadays there is a definite limit for almost every species of duck. You may be allowed to take several of one kind, but only one of another. This means that your game eye must be quick and accurate enough to identify waterfowl at a distance and when they fly unexpectedly into range.

The federal government and many of the states furnish free literature on waterfowl, including silhouettes of the various ducks in flight and color pictures of all the species. Many pamphlets, books and brochures also point out certain characteristics of each species on the water and in flight, to make it easier to recognize.

Before he goes into the marsh or woods, a beginning waterfowl gunner should spend hours poring over the pictures to thoroughly acquaint himself with each kind of duck. Having an experienced guide or partner in the blind with you is a valuable asset when you are training your game eye for waterfowl. The rest comes with experience.

FOCUSING ON DISTANT COVER

Years ago one of my grizzled guides impressed on me that the man who finds more game than the average hunter is the one who can see things at the extreme limit of his vision. He knows that normally he is not going to walk within a few feet of a game animal, so he doesn't concentrate on trying to find it behind the tree or bit of brush nearest him. The odds are that the animals moved out long before he got within rock-throwing distance, so he watches for movement, or outline or a patch of hide, beyond that first line of vegetation and as far as his sight will penetrate into the woods or brush.

You might kick a rabbit, pheasant, quail or larger game out of a brushpile, but the odds are that deer, turkey, wild boar and other such game will be watching for movement that means danger to them more than a few yards away. Large game animals that don't, live short lives.

If you want to know how sharp the vision of many game birds and animals is in the woods, look into thick cover and then look again with 8X binoculars. You will be amazed at how much forest floor, openings, logs and other objects you had not noticed before come into focus. Some game sees that well or better.

You cannot see as well with your eyes as with those binoculars, but you can train your eyes to concentrate on the extreme periphery that is at first clearly seen only with field glasses. When you learn that, you have taken a big step in acquiring a good game eye.

SEEING IN PERSPECTIVE—RANGE FINDING

One of the necessary qualities of a hunter's eye is proper perspective. When I first began hunting elk thirty or more years ago, it was difficult for me to see one even after it had been pointed out by the guide. The valleys were wide and the ridges far apart, yet the rarefied atmosphere was so clear that all objects stood out prominently at long distances. In that clear air I had no sense of how big rocks and trees might be or how far away.

The mountain we were watching for my first elk was so sharply defined that it might have been only a hundred yards away, but the bull pointed out by my guide looked so small that it could have been a brown mosquito with a yellow rump, standing on a blade of grass. Yet even at the great distance, I could see that it was a bull elk with antlers, legs and body, seemingly of microscopic dimensions.

Over the years I finally learned to look for miniature elk and tell how far away they were by their apparent size to my naked eye. I remember writing in my notebook that a hunter might acquire the art of locating elk by sitting on his roof at home and looking for ants crawling around in his yard. On my first hunt, I would have seen an elk only if the animal had measured fifty feet from hoof to antler tips.

Jim Gay had a good suggestion.

"Many of the fellows who hunt with me," he said, "have done most of their shooting in forested sections, and therefore they are poor judges of distance on open range. They can't tell whether an animal is two hundred or eight hundred yards away. One of the best ways I know to correct this is to do a lot of off-season practice with a range finder. Check your naked-eye judgment

I finally learned to look for miniature elk and tell how far away they were by their apparent size to my naked eye.

with the range finder. Use it on horses, cows, dogs, game and people. You'll soon get to where you can judge distance accurately by the apparent size of the creature to your naked eye. This ability is worth a lot when you have made up your mind in a hurry about how far away that big trophy bull or buck is."

Range finders with which I am familiar come in several models. With the less expensive ones you must know the height of the object on which you are aligning for distance, and set this height on a specified dial. The distance dial is then turned until you see two images, one on top of the other. This is good practice with objects of known height, but not as efficient as the finder which operates on the same basis as the range finder on your camera, where the object is sighted through the eyepiece and the focus dial turned until the image is no longer double or shadowed, but stands sharply as a single unit.

A similar finder recently on the market is said to "give direct reading for bullet trajectory, as well as distance, and automatically computes for the hunter how high to aim for any distance up to 500 yards."

Certain scopes are also built to act as range finders. Some have range indicators built into the crosshairs to give an accurate conception of distance between your firing pin and trophy. The scope with the dot is also accurate, once

you know how many inches or feet in diameter the dot covers at a given distance. A 3-inch dot, for instance, covers three inches of diameter every hundred yards. The depth from the chest to the withers of a good mule buck is likely to run between 18 and 21 inches, and if your dot covers this part of the deer in its entirety, you may estimate that he is from 600 to 700 yards away.

These scopes, as well as the range finders, are excellent for helping you to establish distance firmly in your mind, if you take the trouble to make dry practice runs with them between seasons. Your sporting goods dealer can help you make the proper selection of one of these instruments.

Jim also pointed out that an animal usually seems farther away when you are looking downhill, but that is no problem if you have enough experience or practice.

"This may surprise you," Jim continued, chuckling, "but one of the difficulties I have with my hunters is that they can't put their glasses or scope on game even after they have spotted it with the unaided eye. That sounds odd, but it happens many times with inexperienced hunters. When someone asks me how to prepare himself for a hunt, he thinks I'm kidding when I tell him to spend a lot of time looking at objects through his binoculars and scope, so he can handle them efficiently and get them on game in a hurry."

This perspective not only applies to the elk and deer and tyro gunner, but to game a hunter is supposed to be familiar with in his home territory.

Once I went with Ben Waddill and Doc Sapp down to Piney Island on the rim of the Gulf of Mexico, below Tallahassee. While Ben had fished there earlier in the winter, he had noted the flight patterns of the geese and determined that one of the regular lanes of travel lay across a point of the island. That is where we went to set up our stand. The marsh grass and other vegetation were more than tall enough to hide us, so we carried in light, portable stools where we could sit in comfort while we waited.

We had not been there long when we heard the calls of flying Canada geese and spotted a flock of twenty big birds flying directly toward our point, not more than fifty feet above the water. A perfect setup!

The birds winged closer while I crouched tensely in anticipation, thinking that this was much too easy. How wrong a guess that was.

The flock was two hundred yards out, coming dead on, when Doc Sapp suddenly jumped to his feet and started blazing away. The geese flared, climbed and went half a mile around us. Both Ben and I stared at Doc. His look was one of utter surprise.

"How could I miss?" he asked. "They were right on top of us."

"You couldn't have reached one of those birds with a .30/30 rifle," I yelped.

We argued for a while, trying to convince our partner that the birds were much too far out of range, then lapsed again into a period of waiting. It wasn't long before six of the big birds came talking down the same flight lane.

"Now hold your fire," I whispered to Doc, "until they are close enough to kill."

He did better this time. He let the geese get within 175 yards before he leapt to his feet and filled the air with ineffective shot strings.

"What's the matter with you?" Ben snapped.

"I just plain missed," Doc snapped back. "That bird I shot at was close enough to bag with a broom handle."

We settled down to wait again, and after half an hour I glimpsed a third flight of geese coming in. These were low over the water and not making a sound. I cut my eyes at Doc, hoping he would not see them until they were in range. I moved a little closer to Doc and crouched nervously as the geese approached. As luck would have it, about one hundred yards out, a big gander let go with a rolling "hah - onk!" Doc looked up then, saw the flock and tried to jump to his feet. He was not fast enough. I completely engulfed him, pinning his arms to his sides. The way he struggled to free himself, I'll never understand why those Canadas didn't see all that commotion going on in the marsh grass. I held on until they were directly overhead and then released Doc and grabbed for my own gun. The three of us bagged six geese.

Afterward, Doc was apologetic about the first two flights he had fouled up.

"I just didn't understand how really big those honkers are," he said, "until I looked up and saw them directly overhead."

"As long as any game is coming directly toward you," Ben commented dryly, "it's getting in better range all the time. When it starts going in the other direction, then you can start worrying."

Doc's perspective on geese had never been developed until that moment on the tip of Piney Island.

A rather ludicrous example of this happened to me the last time I was in a dove field. The birds were coming in regularly from all directions, and when that is going on, one must be careful not to screw his neck right out of the socket trying to watch them all at once.

There was a lull in the shooting and I looked up from checking the safety catch on my gun to find three doves flying straight toward me, well within range. I threw up my gun and the "birds" simply vanished.

This time I discovered that the "doves" I had seen actually were gnats hovering only a few inches from my eyes.

I scratched my head over that one until a few minutes later when the same thing happened again and this time I discovered that the "doves" I had seen actually were gnats hovering only a few inches from my eyes—a trick in perspective that has fooled me on several occasions.

I am sure that all this must boil down to the ability or experience to be able to instantly identify what one sees and know its relative position. The two eyes that nature gave us—we are lucky it was not just one—are set far enough apart so that we see an object from two angles—a system of triangulation which allows us to judge how far away it is. We begin to learn our judgment of distance almost from infancy and it improves with age. It also grows better with experience, though a few of us never seem to quite reach real efficiency in the matter of distance judging. I have seen hunters in dove fields—and duck blinds, too—shoot at birds so high that no type of scattergun shell could ever be stretched that far, and the birds flew on without even changing the pattern of their flight.

3 The Angler's Eye

SOMEONE once came up with the observation that ten percent of the fishermen catch ninety percent of the fish. This statement was no doubt made by one of those in the ten percent group, or at least by an angler who considered himself one of the elite. And who doesn't think of himself as an expert, if he knows one end of a cane pole from the other?

If this thought has any merit, there must be a reason—perhaps many reasons—why a few of the fishermen catch most of the fish. Among them is knowledge that comes with experience. The Waltonite who devotes several days in every week to fishing, is naturally better at it than the fellow who goes only once or twice each year.

This experience consists of knowing the habits of the species an angler is after, the ability to properly use tackle for either natural or artificial baits, knowledge of the water, weather, temperature and time of day.

One common characteristic I have noticed among all expert anglers is the ability to read a lake, stream, lagoon, estuary or any other type of water. Apparently they can just look at it and know how and where to catch fish. They do this by interpreting what their eyes tell them about the movements of fish, birds, animals and other life around the water. Some of the signs are plainly visible and easily interpreted; many escape a casual eye.

A school of minnows jumping on the surface is one sign that most fishermen recognize, and a few of them do something about. It generally means that larger fish are under, and probably stalking, the school. There is no doubt about it when trout, bass or other game fish begin hitting into a school on the surface.

Over many years Jack Hogg and I caught our share of rainbow trout from two to four pounds out of north Georgia's Lake Burton, by riding the lake and watching for the schools of shad to surface. We would race to a school where the rainbows were striking through it, cast a crystal spoon into the flurry and fish it with an erratic motion just under the shad. If the trout had stopped striking by the time we arrived, then we'd let the spoon sink a few feet and

A school of minnows jumping on the surface generally means that larger fish are under, and probably stalking, the school.

sometimes deeper, and fish it back to the surface. This did not always get a trout, but it produced often enough to keep us in business.

At Lake Lanier, T. B. Willard pulled this same trick with white bass. The schools around his Flowery Branch cove, where he did most of his fishing, were not long in learning the difference between a spoon and live shad and stopped hitting at the sliver of metal. So T. B. switched tactics. He replaced his spoon with a treble hook, heavy enough to cast into the school. Snatching the triple barb through the school usually hooked a minnow. He let it swim with the hook in its side or tail and almost invariably picked up a bass.

We discussed the question of why a fish would pass up healthy members of the school and hit one which was crippled. For this I have only a theory, but will believe it until a better one comes along.

After long years of outwitting and being outwitted by fish, I am reasonably certain that any fish, when hurt, produces a distress signal, probably of such high velocity that were it above the water it would be inaudible to human ears. But other fish hear it and come to investigate, just as a hawk or snake or fox will come to a squeaking rodent. A bass or trout or pike will take a wounded minnow because it is easier to catch. On a Canadian lake in the far north, I have time after time hooked a small pike of four or five pounds in water so clear that I could look down into it and see my hooked fish and its schoolmates, about the same size, swimming along with it. Many times, while I watched, a large northern of eighteen or twenty pounds came charging through the water, passed up the free-swimming pike, which hardly moved out of the way, and hit the hooked fish.

Rather dramatically I tested this theory at a sports and tackle show where the local game department had an exhibit of game fish in several glass tanks. Rainbows in the trout tank were swimming around slowly or hung suspended in the water. With my tongue, I wet the end of my finger and slid it across the glass with just enough pressure to make a squeaking sound. Every fish in the tank turned and charged the tip of my finger, two or three of them bumping the glass so hard that they must have gotten sore noses, and so startling me that I took an involuntary step backward. The squeaking sound produced the same effect at both the bream and black-bass tanks, and I turned to one of the lure manufacturers standing nearby, watching.

"If you could build a squeak or fish distress signal into your lures," I said, "you'd have the best fish catcher ever made."

As far as I know, none of the lure makers have been able to pull off this stunt, though spinners and the "sonic" plugs that make vibrations in the water are usually reliable when fished right.

Schools of threadfins and other bait fish splashing on the surface are the most obvious indications that game fish are around. Another easily recognized manifestation is the sight of circling seagulls or other birds that hover over a school of feeding fish to pick up the morsels where the baitfish are being cut to pieces. This is what the skippers and guides look for on large waters—fresh as well as salt—when they are after feeding fish. A wheeling circle of birds can be seen long distances and unless he has reason to believe that the waters he is in at the moment are certain to produce, almost any skipper will pull in his rigs and head for the collection of birds. Some of the anglers who fish for white bass on the big Santee-Cooper lakes in South Carolina carry powerful field glasses in their boats and spend at least a portion of their hours searching the far horizon for circling sea birds.

Charlie Mooney, who devotes a sizable chunk out of every year fishing for trophy bass in Florida's freshwater lakes and rivers, is strictly a bait fisherman who catches his own shiners in the very lake where he puts out his hooks and corks for trophy fish.

"These baitfish," he told me, "do not occur all over a lake, but only in certain grassy or mossy areas where the water is reasonably shallow, and where other conditions are right. This is the same type of area in which the coots like to feed, so in a new or strange lake I watch for feeding coots and know that I'll find the shiners there."

One of my old angling partners, Ted Henson, can read a lake or stream about as well as anyone I know. His eyes are constantly on the alert for the flash of a minnow, or a telltale swirl in a pocket of grass, or lily pads which sway unnaturally with fish moving through and bumping against the stems. When he sees fry or fingerlings in shallow water and as close as they get against the shore, he has a suspicion that a game fish is lurking somewhere near and

Another sign of game fish is the sight of circling sea gulls or other birds that hover over a school of feeding fish to pick up the morsels where the baitfish are being cut to pieces.

often proves it with a well-placed cast. He can cruise around a lake and tell you the location of every underwater brush top or snag or log heap which is likely to stage a strike.

He has an accurate eye for spotting underwater points by the lay of the shoreline. When the hillside above the lake is steep, chances are good that the angle of the bank is the same in the lake and the water there is deep. He will plug there if the terrain above water is a cliff or strewn with big boulders or logs, for the odds are that these extend on into the lake.

A low, long, flat point reaching into an impoundment more than often runs into the lake at the same angle of slope, all the way to an old creek or river run, where it drops off into deep water. This is an excellent spot for bass, especially if the bottom is rock or hard clay or sand. The fish rest there on the flat where they can move into shallow water at the proper time to feed, or drop off into deep water when danger threatens.

Most white bass, known as stripers, barfish and possibly other names in different places, are taken when they are slashing into a school of minnows on the surface. That and trolling were the methods I used until one of my Arkansas outdoor partners gave me a tip on how to find white bass when they are not making a commotion on the surface.

"One day," said George Purvis, "when I was anchored over a deep hole not far from one of the long points, I noticed that periodically out on the end of the point a school of white bass plowed into a school of threadfins. This would go on for a few minutes, then the lake surface would calm down for a quarter or half an hour, before the bass and shad collided again in almost the same spot.

"This got me to figuring that since shad minnows are notorious movers-around in a lake, then the white bass must be hanging off that point and go into action every time a congregation of shad passed over them. This being the case, why wouldn't they take a lure thrown to them while they waited for the next minnows?

"I eased my boat quietly within casting range of where the feedings had taken place, lowered the anchor gently to the bottom. I threw a small silver spoon to the spot and let it flutter down to the underwater point. When I tightened my line to pick up the spoon, something hit it and I was in business.

"Since then I have caught a lot of white bass by fishing on or close to the bottom where I saw the fish strike on the surface.'

George thus vastly improved his fishing by watching and correctly interpreting what went on around him in the lake.

The same holds true in other types of fishing. One of the most interesting weeks I ever spent was with the late Joe Brooks, internationally known angler, and Ted Williams, one of baseball's all-time greats, and equally skilled with a rod in his hand.

We were on the flats of the Florida Keys, devoting ourselves to the big, powerful bonefish which ranged there. Neither of my partners on this occasion missed much of the action on those flats. Both Ted and Joe had eyes like an osprey and could instantly identify an underwater shadow, so far away that I could not see it, as a cruising shark, barracuda or bonefish. Where I saw a flick of light that could have been a reflection off the top of a wave, they knew it as the mirrored corner of a bonefish tail, where the white fox of the flats stood on its head to get at the tiny crustaceans on which it feeds.

Every movement of fish on the surface, every circling seabird told them volumes, and putting this data through their mental computers gave them the answer on whether to keep poling the boat in search for more fertile fields or to wade and fish.

Although in an entirely different setting, success in freshwater stream fishing depends to a large extent on adding up what you see and acting on the information it gives to you.

When the hillside above the lake is steep, chances are the water there is deep. The wise fisherman will plug there especially if the terrain is strewn with big boulders or logs.

A low, long, flat point reaching into an impoundment more than often runs into a lake at the same angle, all the way to an old creek or river run, where it drops off into deep water. This may be an excellent spot for bass.

Once I made a river trip with a fellow who was as much of a novice as I at float fishing. We had an enjoyable day together, but did not catch any fish. Less than a week later I made a float trip over the same section of water with an old-timer who had been at this for most of the years of his life, and we caught enough fish to load the boat, had we kept them all. I tried to convince myself that this was because the riverman knew where all the fish in that stretch of stream were located, but even if he had, that knowledge would have contributed only partially to our fishing success. A river rolls along with varying moods from day to day, and sometimes almost by the hour, and an experienced angler interprets those moods by what he sees. To the old river fisherman, a kingfisher perched on a limb and watching the water, a minnow flashing in a spot of sunlight, the frantic movements of a frog, a swirl against the bank—all told him something.

Once he held his boat in an eddy and pointed out a small willow tree growing just above the current.

"Boy! Look at that," he said. I looked but did not see anything interesting. "Willow bugs," he explained.

I knew that "willow bug" was the local name for any of several species of mayflies. After a few seconds, one of the insects left the willow bush, flew down and touched the surface as if to take off on an egg-laying spree, and I finally saw the willow loaded with the insects.

"That's nice," I commented. "So what?"

"Watch."

Another bug hit the surface and disappeared in a swirl that came out of the depths.

"We'll back off and fish this eddy," my partner said. "You got anything in your tackle box that resembles a willow bug?"

With both hands, he raised a foot-long rainbow trout above the surface.

I scratched through my box and came up with several ultra-light bladed lures which might have passed as mayflies to a hungry fish.

Apparently the fish in this hole were not too well educated or were very hungry, for we caught bream, catfish and bass up to two pounds in and around the eddy and for a couple of hundred yards down the river.

The smaller a trout stream, the easier it is to solve. You don't need more than one guess to know where the trout are in a branch head that flows from one pothole to another. As it widens and deepens on its way downhill, it takes on character more diversified and more difficult to interpret.

I walked up a north Georgia trout creek with a mountain boy, who obviously had been there before and whose quick eyes did not miss even a shadow in the riffles. The stream was small and none of the pools were much more than knee-deep.

At the first hole he paused and looked over a cluster of boulders at the water's edge.

"Two rainbows live here," he said. "One is nine inches long and t'other about eleven."

At the next pool he added three eight- to nine-inch trout to the score, and at the next, he confided, "Pretty good 'un here, about a foot long and lives by hisself."

"How do you know?" I asked.

"I jest do," he replied, laconically.

"I don't believe it," I stated, flatly.

He grinned. "Then I'll show ye. Look quick, because I don't want t' hurt it."

He rolled his britches up above his knees, his sleeves about the elbows, waded carefully into the pool and felt around the rim of large rocks that flanked the flow of current.

"Look sharp, now," he repeated.

With both hands, he raised a foot-long rainbow above the surface. It flopped once on his outstretched fingers and was gone again to the protection of the boulder.

Although this mountain lad had never heard of "match the hatch," that was the theory he followed in his angling. Until he and I became fast friends and I was able to upgrade his equipment with rod, reel, line and a selection of flies, he fished with a light native bamboo pole he had cut on the creek bank and cured, with white sewing thread, a small shot sinker and small hook. When stick bait, the larvae of the caddis fly, began to appear in his stream, he gathered a tobacco can full of the white grubs that had wrapped themselves in sticks or gravel, and fished them as nymphs down the flow of a riffle and into eddy water. Other favorite nymphs were the hellgrammite, larva of the Dobson fly, which he found around the rocks in and above the water, stone-fly nymphs that he collected from the bottoms of rocks in mid-stream, and the larvae of drone honey bees, wasps and yellowjackets, the collection of which sometimes gave him a painful moment.

His most interesting natural bait was in mayfly season, when he could pluck canfuls of this insect off the trees around the water. By removing the lead-shot sinker from his line, he fished the mayflies dry for some of his most dramatic action.

Capturing some of these nymphs one at the time used up too many of his fishing hours, so he rigged a fine mesh screen on a frame, set it in the flow of the creek and turned over the rocks above it. The screen yielded a rich harvest of insect grubs washed off the upturned stones in the water.

The youngster did not know the names of most of those insects, but he knew the shape and color of each, and could identify the various larvae with the ultimate winged insect. Most important, he knew the time each made its appearance during the season. So when I started him down the artificial route, he was so well versed in natural lore and in the habits of the stream rainbows and brookies, that he took to flyrodding as naturally as I took to his pa's country ham. Because he seldom missed anything happening on a stream, and by pointing out insignificant signs and movements that helped me train my own eye, he was one of my most delightful companions over several years.

I could not resist comparing the mountain lad with a young city-reared trouter who fished a mountain stream not long ago. I am certain his eyes were every bit as sharp as those of the mountaineer; they simply had not been trained in the fine art of observing.

The city boy walked under a hornet's nest hanging over the creek and would have hit it with his backcast had I not happened to catch up with him at that moment and shout a warning. We walked around a deep pool shut in by a rock cliff and he stepped over a motionless copperhead without seeing it. Luckily the snake had only paused in its movement from one location to another and was not coiled with lethal intentions. I amazed the young trouter by pointing out a variety of natural bait and showing him how to "match the hatch"—but have to admit that much of this lore I had acquired from the mountain boy.

The successful taking of fish, however, is not the only pleasure an angler gets out of a day on large or small waters. Hundreds of little dramas and comedies among the wild creatures give him a full and delightful day if he has the eyes to see and the ability to understand what is taking place. It may be the aerial gymnastics of an eagle that makes an osprey drop a fish and then catch it in midair, or a family of otters playing follow the leader down their slide on a muddy bank, or a pair of raccoons amorously nuzzling one another on the end of a log. It may be a doe deer with her fawn standing motionless in the shadows, or a kingfisher diving for its lunch, or a pair of courageous kingbirds whipping a crow or hawk away from their nest.

The outdoors is a never-ending panorama of action and suspense and color to the fisherman who uses his eyes for something besides tying a knot in his leader. Whether he is on the vast ocean, cruising the shore of a lake or river, or wrapped up in emerald vegetation on a singing trout creek, the day will provide greater enjoyment when he learns to see what goes on around him. Not only that, he'll catch a lot more fish.

4 Training the Eyes

TODAY, ONLY a small percentage of us in this rapidly expanding modern world are reared in such places and in such a manner that we have an opportunity to develop the kind of special senses we need if we are to enjoy the outdoors to the utmost.

Compared to our frontier ancestors, we are a hothouse variety of humans and lack keen senses. But the idea of more thoroughly relishing our allotted time in the outdoors appeals to us, and at least some of us are willing to dedicate ourselves to training our eyesight and other senses.

One of the most enjoyable ways I know to accomplish this is to associate with an experienced woodsman. Through his eyes, you may learn to train your own more quickly than by any other method.

Picking the best out of all the competent woodsmen I have known would be most difficult. Some were hunting or fishing partners, some guides, a few simply companions on the trail. Each was different in his way, but all had one thing in common. They were masters in the art of woodsmanship, with keen perception, and were willing to share their experience and knowledge. I learned from every one.

Typical of the breed was George Shuler, who lived all of his almost ninety years in the mountains. Even at that age, his eyes were as bright as marbles and never missed anything that went on about him. He knew the mountain coves and creeks and ridges flanking his cabin on Jack's River, twenty miles from the nearest paved road, as well as I know the nooks and crannies of my own backyard. Once I came by his cabin with a pocketful of butternuts I had picked up along one of the game trails. I asked a foolish question.

"Did you know about that tree?"

His gray eyes smiled.

"Did you get them from under that butternut tree up where the old chimney fell down, or the one over by the ford of the river, or that group of trees up in the Pounding Mill flat?"

He turned one of the nuts around in his hand, studying it.

"I'd say it came from the tree near the old chimney."

"Now how would you know that?" I asked.

"Nuts are bigger on that tree and shaped a mite different," he said.

I thought he was pulling my leg and later checked for myself. There wasn't much difference, but it was there and George had noticed it.

Once he told me about a patch of rare yellow violets along one of the creeks about a mile from his house and I brought home a few for milady's rock garden.

Being with George in the woods or on a trail was an education in how one should use his eyes. His were constantly on the alert. He saw every track that crossed a trail, every disturbed pebble. Not an ant moved or a hawk sailed overhead that he didn't notice. Slyly he would point out where a deer had skidded a sliver of moss off a rock, or a bobcat had crouched, or a coon had padded across a soft spot in the trail. Almost before I knew it, I was walking along with my eyes glued to the ground, trying to identify a few marks on my own. Then George would say, "There's a hen turkey yonder. She just stepped off the trail."

That would make me realize that while a fellow can read a world of interesting gossip by keeping his eyes glued to the earth, unless he gives them a constant change of scenery, he misses plenty, too.

I began to watch George. He would take in a section of trail at a glance, then shift his look to the farthest perimeter of his vision, then to the treetops and the sky overhead. He watched both sides of the trail and occasionally gave some attention to the direction from which we had come.

"A body ought to keep up with what goes on behind him," he explained when he looked back and caught my eye.

The mountain man did this subconsciously and not with any applied effort, though I am sure my efforts were conscious when I tried to imitate him. He moved through the woods with great deliberation, and never followed a mountain trail as though he were running a footrace, yet we could cover a tremendous amount of territory in a day.

Once I was at the cabin when another mountaineer dropped by to sit and chew the fat for a spell. They talked of weather and other inconsequential things and after a pause, George asked, "Did you kill that gobbler on the big flat above Rough Creek the other morning?"

"How'd you know I was huntin' there?" the visitor countered.

"Seen yore tracks," George said.

"Didn't hear him," the mountain neighbor replied, and the conversation went back to less significant subjects.

"How did you guess it was his track and that he was gobbler hunting?" I asked, after the visitor had left.

"Didn't guess," George replied. "If it wasn't that fellow, it was some 'un who had borrowed his shoes. No two shoes make the same kind of marks on the ground. The tracks were only two or three hours old when I seen them about the middle of morning. There ain't no possible reason he could be on that flat at that time of day in the spring unless he was turkey huntin', and I'd a-knowed that if I hadn't seen where he stopped to listen and put the butt of his gun on the ground."

George had the unlimited patience of any real woodsman, without which one cannot learn to use his eyes and other sense organs in such a way that they are most valuable to him in the outdoors. Not only was he always unhurried, but often he remained in one spot for a long time until he interpreted what he had seen or what was happening that he could not see.

If I had not already learned this lesson in deliberation from wild turkey hunting or from George, I am sure I would have had my most valuable training in this particular asset when I hunted elk with Phonograph Jones in Wyoming's Yellow Creek Basin above the South Fork of the Shoshone.

Jonesy was another fellow who stayed in the woods until he was more than ninety years old. In his early years he was an associate of Buffalo Bill Cody, and later he spent many winters trapping in the remote and isolated Thorofare.

I was on many hunts with him. We took our last trip together when he was eighty-five years young. In our party were two hunters, two guides and Jonesy, who went along as cook.

Horseback and afoot, I covered considerable territory around camp, trying to find a good bull, and one afternoon I persuaded Jonesy to forget his kitchen chores and hunt with me. We rode a couple of miles up a long, wooded valley, ground-hitched our horses in a patch of heavy grass, just short of a high rim overlooking the basin, and sat down with our backs to a boulder to glass the creeks, ridges, hillsides and scattered patches of timber in the big territory spread out below us. This was shortly after noon, when very little game is moving. With our binoculars, we covered what portion of the valley we could see, most thoroughly, saw little more of interest than a couple of ravens flying across one of the high tops, and I made a move to get to my feet and go after the horses.

"What's your hurry?" Phonograph asked quietly.

"No elk in this pocket," I replied.

"Don't bet on it," he said. "We are out of the wind here, the sun is warm, our horses are happy in all that grass, so let's park a while longer and look."

I wanted to go find an elk somewhere, but I reluctantly took my seat again to continue glassing what I considered empty country. We must have been there an hour before Jonesy touched my arm.

"See that little creek valley coming in from the left? About halfway up it there's a scattered clump of spruce. Just beyond that largest tree is a low, grassy mound with a brown patch of something just behind it. See if you can make it out?"

I could see the brown patch, but it looked like the topside of a boulder. I watched it for a few minutes and was about to shift my binoculars in another direction when something moved. The top side of a bull elk came instantly into focus, including the antlers, which were so camouflaged in a pattern of tree limbs that neither of us had made them out until the animal turned its head. A closer search through the glasses revealed a cow lying on the slope beyond the patch of timber. Later in the afternoon when the animals began to move, four more cows, for a total of six elk, came out of that timbered patch where we had not been able to spot a living creature in our first hour of glassing the valley.

In the meantime, we had found another little band of elk that showed up in a line of willows and alders along the main creek, a coyote that crossed the ridge below us and a couple of mule deer, one with a nice rack, lying in a sunny spot higher on the ridge. The place was alive with game. Before the afternoon was over, we looked at six good bulls—none with as large a rack as we wanted—and a big bull moose that moved into the picture.

Old Jonesy had given me a very valuable lesson in patience, one that I have used time and again in hunting elk, as well as other game animals and birds. I am convinced that the ability to stay put and sit still is a necessary factor in developing a good game eye.

WATCHING THE BIRDS

One of the quickest ways I know for any person to train his eyes—and ears—is by taking up the study of birds. Not only does this help sharpen your senses, but through it you attain a knowledge that will give you many delightful hours afield, whether you are hunting, fishing, or following some other outdoor activity unrelated directly to our feathered citizens.

With the hundreds of species, including those which pass by twice a year in migration, and with many of them similar in habits and coloration, you must develop an alert eye to be able to identify a bird that flashes across your vision. This quick evaluation is helpful in many kinds of hunting.

Those with experience in such things say that the best place to start learning the birds is at home. You can begin with those you see on the lawn. Keep a bird book with color pictures close at hand for quick identification of those feathered visitors to your premises.

One of the surest places I have found for seeing a variety of birds is around a bird feeder, suspended from a tree limb or otherwise installed near a window where I can stand and watch unobserved. This gives me plenty of time to study the color charts and select the species to which the bird on my feeder belongs.

I use two types of feeders—one holding cracked grain for the seed-eating birds and the other filled with suet for those species that live on insects. Both of those feeders are busy spots in the backyard.

After you have identified the birds common around your residence well enough to recognize two or three dozens of species from a distance, then is the time to venture farther afield. Your best bet here is to go with someone experienced in bird identification. You learn more quickly by having various members of the feathered clan pointed out to you, so that you may study the identifying characteristics of the bird in flight, the way it perches and its notes as well as its colors. You learn in this way to recognize it under many conditions.

A number of different pocket guides are available. You will get more pleasure and learn faster with one of these as an item of your equipment.

Many species are such shy, furtive creatures that they are seldom seen even by experienced bird students. Knowing the locations where these birds may be found, and seeking them out, is fine practice for helping to hone your game eye.

You won't become a professional ornithologist in a week or a month or a year, but the more you get into bird study, and watch the antics and dramas of the avian world, the more you will be fascinated by it. To become an expert in bird identification in the field requires continuous practice, and you may be assured that in addition to the pleasure you get out of it, you are at the same time training your eyes and ears for seeing and hearing just about everything that goes on in the outdoors.

USING BINOCULARS

One of the items of equipment essential to bird students, as well as to most hunters of big-game animals, is a pair of good binoculars.

Amazing as it may seem, not many people know how to use field glasses. Hand a man who is not familiar with them a pair of binoculars and tell him to look at a small object, and the odds are that even though he sees it with his naked eye, he will find difficulty in picking it up through the glass. The more practice you have, the more proficient you will become in the use of field glasses.

These are, in reality, an extension of your vision. Watching birds or game or whatever with this assistance, helps you to identify and become acquainted with every part of the anatomy of a bird or animal, so that when a large portion of the creature is hidden, eventually you can spot and identify what you see without the use of glasses.

When you add these to your bird watching or hunting gear, I suggest the best binoculars that your pocketbook can afford. With the proper care, they will last a lifetime.

The price of such glasses naturally depends on the quality of material used in them and the workmanship in putting them together, and generally ranges from $25 to more than $500.

Just what are the specifications of a "good" glass for either bird study or hunting? Factors taken into consideration should include power of magnification, field of vision, degree of illumination, weight and size. A person inexperienced in such matters is likely to want all of the magnification he can get. This is a mistake. A 12- or 15-power glass is generally much too large and heavy for fast or continuous operation, and long uninterrupted use will strain your eyes. On the other hand, very small binoculars usually have a narrow field of vision that limits their effectiveness.

Recommending any particular glass suitable to all individuals is impossible. For my own use I have found the 7 X 35 binoculars most practical. These are not too heavy around my neck on an all-day trip; they do not tire my eyes when I look through them for long periods at a time, and they cover a field large enough so that I can quickly find a bird or animal I have seen with the naked eye. The degree of illumination is also great enough for use in the dim light of early morning or late afternoon.

One mistake the purchaser of his first pair of field glasses is likely to make is buying a pair on which each eyepiece must be focused separately. Much preferred is the focusing arrangement that moves both eyepieces when turned, but with an adjustment on one eyepiece for your own degree of astigmatism. This adjustment is marked off in plus and minus numbers. I am familiar enough with my glass so that I can set the adjustable eyepiece at the right spot without having to focus it for clearness each time I look through it. This gets me more quickly on a bird or animal.

The trick here is to keep your eye on the object you wish to watch or study with the increased power and to aim the glasses as you would put the cross-hairs of a scope on it. If you miss with the first try, find the object with your naked eye and "aim" again with the binoculars. Practice makes perfect.

When hanging around your neck by a strap, binoculars sometimes are a nuisance if you crouch or bend over. They swing down against a rock or limb,

Hold binoculars as still as you can. Sit down, if possible, steady elbows on your knees, and brace forefingers against your forehead.

For more precision sighting, sharpen focus of your binoculars carefully, and brace them on a log or some other solid object.

which doesn't do them any good. My hunting friend, Jim Gay, remedies this by attaching a piece of long-stretching elastic from his glasses around his back, to hold them against his body when he bends over. Yet the elastic has enough stretch so that he can pick the binoculars up to his eyes with little more effort than if they dangled free.

Good field glasses increase your enjoyment of the outdoors and at the same time hasten the development of sharper-than-average vision that many woodsmen spend a lifetime acquiring.

USING A CAMERA

Another good assist in improving your consciousness of what goes on beyond the realm of walls and doors and windows is the camera.

Kenneth Rogers, who was photographer for the Atlanta (Georgia) *Journal and Constitution* for more than forty years, was one of the best outdoor picture takers of my acquaintance. Over the four decades I worked with him, we went on countless hunting, fishing, camping and story-gathering trips together. He more than anyone taught me the importance of scene setting and angle and foreground to give a photograph depth and character.

Once Kenneth and I discovered something in one of his pictures that gave me an idea. He snapped a black and white shot of bird dogs on point, with two hunters walking in behind them. When he printed the picture and we were looking at it back in the studio, we were surprised to discover that it showed half a dozen quail crouched in the grass in front of the dogs. We had not seen them while the photo was being taken, but I am sure they never would have escaped the attention of some of my old outdoor guides who seldom missed seeing any creature within range of their vision.

Another time when I was pussy-footing upwind through a western forest, my eye caught a movement and made out a doe deer partially screened by a clump of trees. Very carefully, I slid my camera around, focused it and made a couple of pictures. I glanced down to roll my film and check again for values on the light meter built into the camera, and when I looked up again the doe was gone.

My picture was a 2¼-by-2¼ transparency, and after it came back from the processer, I blew it up on a 4½-foot screen, which is the way I look at all the transparencies I make. You could have knocked me over with a duster made out of doe hair, for there in the picture stood a better-than-average buck, outlined even more boldly than the doe. And I had not even been aware of the critter. I must have concentrated my entire attention on the doe after seeing the flick of her ear or tail or whatever movement she made.

Each of those photos was slightly humiliating to a fellow who prides himself on his ability to go through the woods and see at least most of the things that are there. It also activated my thinking further. From that time on, when the movement of some bird or animal caught my attention, I made myself take my eyes off it long enough to study the terrain on all sides. That is not easy to do, even though you know it is one way of training your senses. Until those two photos came along, I had been so intrigued with my ability to spot one creature that I forgot to look for two—or more.

I bagged my biggest elk because I forced myself to take my eyes off one good six-pointer and look for others around it. By studying the terrain very carefully, I made out three cows standing motionless and then a tremendous animal so screened by trees that about all I could see were those horizontal lines Jim Gay had called to my attention.

Then the bull stepped for an instant into a little clearing about the size of a clothes closet. Another step and he would have been gone, and I am sure I never would have spotted him at all, had I not been looking directly at the spot. The head was crowned with massive antlers—or so I thought.

I put my sights in the right place and the bull went down. I am certain that I owed the kill to those two photographs that had made me study the areas around the game I first saw. I am equally sure that the bull would have gone into the record books, except for one thing. He carried only one tremendous antler on his port side. As a matter of interest, when we skinned him out, we found only one testicle on the same side as the antler. No biologist has ever been able to explain that one to me.

RANGE FINDER

A third instrument I have found valuable when I am in the process of trying to condition my eyes for a hunting trip is a range finder. One of the most difficult things for almost any novice hunter to do is correctly judge distance, especially under conditions strange to him, such as wide open spaces or high, rarefied atmosphere. If an animal is six hundred yards away and the tyro gunner shoots for two hundred, he has little chance of scoring.

You might think that such an occurrence could never happen to a fellow, even on his first hunt, but it can. A few years ago I was on a big-game hunt in the Canadian Rockies with a friend who was not exactly in the rooky class, since he had been on enough big-game trips to know at least most of the ropes. We were after sheep and hunted hard for trophy heads, which seemed somewhat scarce in that immediate area.

One afternoon we hunted up a big valley, pausing frequently to glass the heights on both sides, and near the head of the valley spotted a couple of ewes with lambs and a small ram with a three-quarter curl. We looked them over a while and were about to move on when the guide discovered a second ram lying down. Only the top of his head above the eyes was visible, but that portion of the horns we could see looked tremendous.

Even though the sheep had seen us, we pulled the horses out of sight, tied them and climbed afoot through a canyon to where we would be on a level with the sheep and could study our best approach to get near enough for a shot.

When we considered that we were high enough to peep again, we inched back to the rim on our bellies. The sheep were where we had last seen them, but the big ram was on his feet, and I did not need my glasses to tell me that he was a beauty. The guide and I were looking him over anyway and paying no attention to my partner. I almost jumped out of my hide when the fellow's gun went off almost in my ear. It couldn't have scared me any more if I had known he was shooting at me instead of the ram. Before we could stop him, he shot a second time and the band of sheep disappeared as though it had been wiped out of the picture.

"What do you think you're shooting?" I snapped. "An antiaircraft weapon?"

"That ram was well within range," he countered.

"What do you call 'within range'?"

"Hell," he said, "it couldn't have been more than a couple of hundred yards."

I glanced at the guide and he had a funny expression around his eyes, but he didn't say anything. Later we discussed the distance across the head of that valley. My estimate would have been around five hundred yards, and our guide grunted at that.

"We were three quarters of a mile away from that critter," he declared. "He'd a had to lob one in to reach it."

I am sure it was not a very tactful thing to do, but I gave my friend a range finder for Christmas, with a note that if he continued to hunt the big open spaces, he might find it useful. Then, on second thought, I gave myself one too, and have never regretted it. Between the gunning seasons I do a lot of hunting through the range finder. With it, of course, any animal, including cows, horses, dogs and people, is legal game. It is rather amusing to estimate the distance to a cow grazing in the pasture and then check on it with the range finder to see how far I might have missed, had I been after my winter meat and that cow was the only creature left on the range. By playing this brand of solitaire, I have learned plenty about distance and perspective.

Two kinds of range finders are available. With one, you have to know the height of the object you are judging before you can get your distance. This is not as satisfactory as the finder that works on the same principle as the distance indicator on your camera, in which you see two images when your subject is out of focus and only one when you bring it into the proper focus for your lens.

TRAINING THE EYES AT HOME

One of the ways I have tried to consciously train my senses is by watching the actions of the birds and other creatures around my house. A dozen species, including a covey of quail and several squirrels, congregate to feed on the cracked grain I scatter around the feeder just outside the window of my study. Those birds and squirrels react differently to each of the various types of disturbance. A hawk, crow or other large bird flying overhead will send all of the songsters, except the quail, in wild flight for the protection of a thicket bordering the backyard. The bobwhites crouch motionless and watch until the large bird has gone, and then go back to feeding. The squirrels either go on feeding or hop close to a trunk of one of the trees. One by one, the smaller birds return.

I do not have to see it to know when a strange dog comes into the yard. Every bird vacates the feeding area, most of them merely flying up into the trees above it. The squirrels disappear and the quail take off for the honeysuckle thicket along the tree. As long as the dog stays in the yard, if not too close, one or two songsters at a time will drop quickly down off a limb, catch a snack or two and fly into the tree again. When the dog moves on, they come back to eat as a group, except the quail. The squirrels perch on a tree limb until bowser is out of sight.

The sudden appearance of a person will send the birds flying, but the squirrels pay little attention unless the human walks through the feeding area, in which case they retire to the safety of a limb to sit and usually chatter until the ground is safe again. They are first back to the dinner table and the birds come in a few at a time.

Just like those in the backyard, the birds in the wild react differently to different situations, and many times an experienced outdoorsman can read what is happening in the woods by the actions of various species. To a farmer, circling vultures may mean that he has lost one of his cows or that it is down and sick. To a big-game guide, a congregation of ravens, circling or in the trees, might indicate that a wounded animal escaped the hunter before it died, was found by the ravens, which were driven off the kill by an animal such as a bear or coyote. Crows in a ruckus-raising flock may mean a hawk or owl or some unusual situation in which animals are involved. One southern swamp hunter told me that he found a grove of oak trees full of fox squirrels by following the sound of screaming jaybirds, with whom the squirrels were competing for food.

By observing and investigating the actions of the wilderness citizens, we can make long strides in the training of an active and interpretive eye that will give us much pleasure in the outdoors, no matter what our reason for being there.

5 Tracks and Sign

A GOOD outdoor eye goes much further than merely the ability to see animals or birds. Sometimes the success of a hunting, fishing, photography or bird-watching trip depends upon an individual's correct interpretation of faint claw or pad prints on the earth, an upturned pebble, a vine pulled from its moorings, scuffed leaves, or a combination of those and other sign. There are times when a man's life is worth no more than what those marks he reads on the ground mean to him.

Many outdoorsmen I know rely to a great extent on what a stretch of wilderness tells them by its sign. Often turkey hunters and big-game hunters scout a country in advance of the season and then concentrate their efforts in that territory where tracks, droppings, horned trees, browsed bushes or vines, and scratching show an abundance of animals and birds.

It is second nature with an experienced woodsman to devote at least a part of his attention to the terrain over which he walks or rides, and make a mental note of everything from disturbed earth to a rock or stick or even a log that seems to be out of place.

One of the keenest fellows I ever knew at seeing and interpreting signs was Roy Glasgow. Roy was a mountain man all his life, and his country was the lofty Absaroka Range that crowds up against the boundary of Yellowstone National Park in western Wyoming. His qualities as a frontiersman must have been equal to those of the explorers and trappers of a century and a half ago, who were woodswise enough to keep their scalps in a country full of cantankerous Indians and short-tempered silvertips.

There was not a broken twig, bent blade of grass or mark on the earth that Roy did not observe and interpret. He had the patience of a frontier mountain man: if he saw a movement in the forest, he would sit or stand motionless until he knew what it meant.

One of the few times the old guide ever got in trouble was by not properly heeding sign. He told me that he had ridden alone and without his rifle to the top of a high ridge to locate some rams for a couple of sheep hunters he had in tow. Along the crest of the ridge he saw tracks of a sow grizzly and two cubs, but the tracks were several hours old and the bears were traveling, so he paid the sign but slight attention.

He ground-hitched and left his horse to graze, and worked his way toward a small clump of trees at the head of a rock slide. He was standing below the tree clump, glassing the open country ahead when the grizzly roared behind him. Roy swung around and she was right on top of him, her mouth open. Just as she hit him, he shoved the binoculars in his hand down her throat with all the power in his right arm.

The speed and weight of the bear carried them head over heels down the slope to the upper end of the rock slide. In the scramble, she crushed the binoculars, spat them out and then clamped down on the guide's leg. His heavy leather chaps, plus a couple of cartridges and a cigarette lighter in his pocket, prevented her from biting all the way through and breaking a bone or severing his leg completely. She flung him down the rock slide and went back to her cubs.

Roy had a chewed-up hand and hurt from the mauling he had received, but was curious enough, before he rode back to camp, to know how he had misjudged the tracks of the bears. They led at an angle away from the clump of trees and this had given him the idea that they had gone on. Then out on the slope, they turned at right angles and came back to the thicket, where the sow had lain down with her cubs until Roy happened along.

"And you can bet your best saddle blanket," he said, "that forever after when I've seen silvertip tracks that fresh, I take a few more pains to find out that the critters making them are not close by, or to be ready for them if they are."

Although I have wandered through the forests and swamps and across the plains all over this continent for most of my life, I must admit that I find it difficult to devote the proper amount of attention to sign when I am concentrating on trying to see game, or to watching for game when I become interested in tracks. It's like one of my outdoor partners, Paul Fedder, says. Paul has downed many a whitetail buck and he claims that the reason many deer hunters are not successful is that they keep their eyes on the ground for sign when they should spend at least a part of their time looking elsewhere.

"I've been in the woods," he states, "with guys who hunt tracks like they could shoot and eat them. They spend the day with their eyes glued to the good earth. A man should hunt mostly with his head up."

Paul's theory is that tracks are important when you are trying to locate the mountain or swamp where a big buck lives, but after you know he's there, you have a better chance to see him if you spend at least a part of your time looking farther away than the ground at your feet.

I learned that the hard way, when I hunted moose with Bill Bousfield in western Ontario in mid-December. The weather was around forty-five degrees below zero, the snow twelve to fifteen inches deep and like coarse powder. No matter what kind or how many layers of clothes I put on, there was no way to keep my Cracker blood from congealing unless I stayed on the move.

Moose tracks were everywhere and the trick was to follow a trail in slow motion until you saw a bull grazing ahead, or got close enough to jump one that was bedded down.

We had found the tracks of an especially large moose that moved around on a peninsula jutting into the lake, and I spent some time trying to catch up with this particular animal. One afternoon, Bill and I had gone in different directions and I was stalking through a thicket where the snow was a little deeper than usual, and came across a set of very fresh tracks, spaced far enough apart to indicate a big animal making long strides.

I put my nose to the trail like a Walker hound—without the bark—and followed the tracks that zigzagged through the forest, until they arrived at a big, sprawling, brushy top of a wind-thrown tree. There the tracks went *under* the treetop, instead of around it.

When the realization dawned that I had followed the trail of a snowshoe rabbit, traveling through the deep snow with leaps just far enough apart that they had every appearance of being made by a moose, I stood up and laughed aloud at myself—which was the wrong thing to do. The brush crashed off to my left and I got a glimpse of a bull disappearing into the thickets.

Had I been watching ahead instead of having my nose in the rabbit tracks, I might have bagged a good trophy.

Once in Alaska I met a man who had failed to properly interpret sign. To convince me how badly he had failed, he took off his shirt and showed me an ugly scar where a huge chunk of meat had been torn out of his back.

He and his wife had cruised in their small boat out to the peninsula to hunt. From Kanatak they went west, pulling their boat into sheltered bays to hunt the surrounding countryside. They were especially interested in a big peninsula brownie.

They spent one afternoon with high-powered rifles in a series of low hills above a long arm where the boat was anchored. They found no bear tracks, but the hills were working alive with ptarmigan, so the next morning he left his .30/06 on the boat and while his wife was preparing breakfast, took his .22 out to get a few of the birds. A couple of hundred yards from the boat, he crossed tracks left by a large bear, stopped and looked at them, wondering why he had not seen them there the afternoon before.

He soon found out. They were much fresher than he thought. He came over a little rise and met the brownie face to face. Before he could move the bear charged, knocking him down. The .22 flew off to one side.

"The only weapon I could think of was my knife," he recalled. "I reached for it and that probably saved my life."

The bear hit at the movement of his hand, and ripped the hunk of flesh out of the back of his shoulder. The blow turned him over, the brownie gave him another blow and he lost consciousness.

When he came to, the bear was gone. Weak from loss of blood, he staggered and crawled back to the boat. His wife packed the hole to stop the flow of blood and brought him to the nearest settlement more dead than alive.

Misreading the age of that bear sign came near costing him his life.

Identifying tracks and learning to read them can be fun. Likely spots to find the best impressions left by raccoons, otters, opossums, fox, muskrats and squirrels and many of the birds are mud bars along the creeks and rivers, in the soft earth of trails, logging roads or any open ground not covered with vegetation or leaves. The track of each species is distinctive, and once you become thoroughly acquainted with it, you can recognize a track if only a portion of it is visible.

Many publications occasionally carry drawings of animal tracks and one publishing company puts out a pocket field guide on the subject. This is an informative booklet for any beginning outdoorsman to have in his pocket or his kit. It will afford him many hours of entertainment and add greatly to his store of animal lore.

Combinations of animal tracks are more than mere prints on the ground. Often they tell an interesting story. Once on an elk hunt in Arizona's Coconino National Forest, I was walking along a ridgetop and came across fresh mountain-lion tracks in the snow. The leisurely stride of the cat showed that he was unalarmed and I kept peering ahead, trying to see him.

I came to a spot where the lion had crouched, then bounded forward with giant strides. I was sure he had discovered me on his trail until another set of tracks told where a porcupine, waddling along, had seen or heard the big cat and tried to reach the safety of a tree. He almost made it. The lion had stood on his hind feet and appeared to have flipped the porcupine off the tree trunk into the snow, caught it a few feet farther on, turned it over, ripped open the belly and ate the insides. The cat had calmly walked away from the spot, with no sitting down in the snow or other indication that he had run afoul of a porcupine quill.

Tracks and other sign often convey a message or forecast, as well as a story. In Wyoming's Thorofare, you will always know that winter has set in by the arrangement of tracks in the many trails. The hoofprints show that deer are moving toward the high passes that slope down to the South Fork country where the herds winter. The bands of elk travel in the other direction, many of them to winter in and around the big-game refuge in Jackson Hole.

The movement of animals and birds often presages a storm as effectively as a falling barometer—or your aching corns. Through their systems of stations, the weather people keep up with the high-pressure and low-pressure areas and fronts. So do the wild creatures, which apparently have something akin to built-in barometers. By watching the storm fronts along the Atlantic seaboard, I can always predict when we will have a good flight of ducks to the lakes and rivers around my home in middle Georgia. When a northeaster is blowing down the coast in the direction of Carolina and Georgia marsh and hinterland, the waterfowl move from a few to a few hundred miles inland, depending on how severe the storm will be, even though there may not be a cloud in the sky at the time.

Once on a hunting trip early in the season, when we expected to find the deer on top of the highest ridges, we climbed our tongues out without finding fresh sign, until my partner, an accomplished woodsman, suggested that since we knew the bucks and does were plentiful in that country, we try the lower coves and creek bottoms.

This we did and found deer all over the place. About the third time we flushed some does and a small buck out of thickets, my companion began to look worried.

"We'd better go to camp," he suggested, "and batten down all the hatches."

"With all these critters running over us?" I asked.

"We are in for some real weather," he stated.

And we were. Before the day was out, a near blizzard set in and for a while it appeared that we might be snowed in for the winter.

The actions of a bird or animal will often tell you something if you know how to read the movements. I am pleased with myself when I can.

I was turkey hunting in the Tennessee mountains with a couple of friends. We knew the country well and before we left the road at daylight, we mapped the approximate course each of us would take through that portion of the big watershed where we hunted. That would keep us from conflicting with one another, should either of us make contact with a gobbler.

One of my friends was an expert turkey hunter, the other a novice. Call them Billy and Phil. Phil had never bagged a gobbler, and Billy was anxious to help him break the long losing streak, so they decided to hunt together.

I crept down the ridge I had chosen, pausing to call and listen, then move ever so slowly to another calling point. Around the middle of morning, as I slipped stealthily to the crest of a high point on the ridge, I jumped two deer out of a thicket. I was on the downwind side, had not made any great amount of noise and they were more curious than afraid. They stood and looked me over for a moment, presumably identified me as a man and went loping off under the contour of the hill in the general direction of a low gap below where I stood.

I dismissed the incident from my mind and would have forgotten it completely, except that in a few minutes the deer were back, bounding along approximately the same course over which they had departed. One of them paused below me to look back before they went out of sight up the slope.

The only logical conclusion was that something below me had spooked them, and from their actions, it almost had to be a human. From the lay of the land as I remembered it, the easiest crossing of the creek valley between the ridge I was on and the one Phil and Billy had gone down, was opposite the shallow gap below me. The odds were that for some reason my two partners had crossed over to my ridge, and the deer had seen them climbing into the low gap.

I gave the coarse yelp of a young gobbler on my box and then sat down to wait and see how right my diagnosis had been. Sure enough, the plaintive note of a hen came back from the gap. The hen calls were repeated at intervals for half an hour or more, but I did not reply, and after awhile I caught a glimpse of Billy coming up the ridgetop trail, with Phil a few steps behind. They had run into other hunters on their ridge and so crossed over to the one they knew I was on.

The actions of the deer had given their presence away, and I wondered how often a turkey gobbler had read sign similar to that and understood it enough to scare him away.

The actions of the deer had given their presence away, and I wondered how often a turkey gobbler had read sign similar to that I had seen and understood it enough to scare him out of the country.

REMEMBERING LANDMARKS

The reason any capable outdoorsman seldom gets lost is because he notes sign—including landmarks. I maintain, and there are many who agree, that outside the primitive tribes, few humans are blessed with a sense of direction. The man who spends much of his time outdoors learns to make a mental note of everything he sees and files it away in the back of his mind. When he walks into some nook of the forest that he has seen before, every feature of it falls into place in the picture he has kept in his mind. The rock cliff is still there, with a crescent scar where a chunk of rock has lost its moorings, and the old chestnut snag with a double-barrel hollow, and the huge buckeye tree that leans at an angle as though it were about to fall, and the open character of the woods. He was there only once, but these features stuck in the back of his memory.

A woodsman subconsciously remembers the direction of the main range and how the ridges run, the flow of the streams, which side of the road or trail he is on, the near and distant boundaries of the region through which he travels. He conceives the entire area as a map, and if caught by darkness or a storm, he goes on instruments—which means a good compass to help him keep on course.

Once on a cloudy day in the Okefenokee Swamp on the Georgia-Florida line, a fishing companion and I followed a dim water trail that turned and twisted through the drowned wilderness, until we were completely turned around.

This one-third-of-a-million-acre swamp is one spot I have found where—with very few exceptions—one portion very nearly resembles every other portion. It contains distinctive terrain, such as the cypress forest, "prairies" of floating semiland, open lakes and islands, and these are laid over it in a mosaic pattern. Except for the scattered islands, the entire area is covered with water that averages deeper than you or I would care to walk in.

The day, which had been overcast, developed into one filled with misty rain and my partner said, "We'd better get the hell out of here."

"I'm with you," I agreed. "Which way?"

"I have no idea," he admitted.

On our trip into the interior, my boat mate had observed what all the local swampers know—that although the Okefenokee has the appearance of a vast, motionless lake, a current flows through it, roughly from north to south. It is evident in the leaning grass and other underwater vegetation. We also knew that we were somewhere north of Billy's Lake, where we had launched our boat.

We worked our way out of that morass by following the flow of the water. It was not easy, because we had to backtrack a few times and paddle around thickets and log heaps, but when we hit the main run going into Billy's Lake, they probably heard my sigh of relief all the way to the landing.

It was my partner's observation that the inland sea did have a current that got us safely out of what might have been an unpleasant night or two in the swamp.

READING A TRAIL

Men who have spent their lives watching tracks and sign, and through experience have learned how to read them correctly, develop a knack for tracking and interpreting what the tracks mean. I have witnessed some remarkable examples of this ability.

I was with an old trapper who had one of his traps pulled loose from a log where it was not anchored too securely. For half a mile he trailed the animal with the trap on its foot, by the disturbed leaves, the faint marks made by the steel at the bases of small trees where the animal had passed, and rocks skinned of a fragment of moss.

We were traveling fast, but probably never would have caught up, had not the trap finally lodged in the forks of a sapling that branched just above the ground, in such a manner that the big bobcat in the trap could not pull it free. My trapper finally collected his pelt.

Another time a couple of our guides tracked a hunter lost from our camp, and amazed me as well as him by an accurate account of every move he had made from the time he left the main trail until he got back to camp.

We were returning from a spike camp and a member of our party rode ahead to the main camp to tell the cook he would have extra faces around the supper table.

Our hunting companion came to a fork in the trail and having no idea which branch was right, wisely gave his mount its head. It was the first trip the horse had made into that country and he did not know any more about it than the hunter. At the junction where they paused, the main trail angles off a steep bank and crosses a rocky creek bottom, while the secondary pathway continues on around the contour and at this point is wider and more inviting than the main trail. It was only natural that both the man and his horse should make the wrong choice.

Our hunter was not in the main camp when we arrived, did not show up that night, so the next morning two of the guides set out to find him. They backtracked along the main trail until they saw where one horse had turned off up the side trail. One of the guides knelt on the ground to study the tracks.

"This is him, all right," he said. "I remember how those horseshoes look. I put them on last week."

Now to a layman like you or me, the print made by one horseshoe would look exactly like the print of all other horseshoes, but a fellow familiar with it can look at a track and recognize the size, shape and possibly the make of the shoe.

When twilight began to fill up the valleys, my friend who had ridden off the main trail began to suspect that he might be lost. He was about to turn back when he came upon a tent left by one of the outfitters for use as a spike camp later in the season. He spent the night there and the next morning, following the suggestion I had made that a lost man could usually find his way back to a trail, road or settlement by following the flow of a stream, he turned his horse down the creek, found the main trail crossing and rode into camp around noon. He missed the fellows trailing him, since they were following his tracks on the trail that paralleled the creek along a high bench several hundred yards from the stream.

Late in the afternoon the two guides rode into camp. I met them at the corral to announce that the wandering hunter was safe.

"Yeah, we know," one of the guides said laconically, "we trailed him here."

After they unsaddled their horses, they came up to the tent for a drink.

"I found a place to spend the night," the hunter who had been lost told them.

One of the guides grinned.

"We sort of kept up with you," he said. "When you got to the tent, you got off, tied your horse to a tree and went inside. You decided to spend the night there, so you went back to your horse, took your gun out of the saddle scabbard, leaned it against a tree, and put your horse in the pole corral without taking off the saddle.

"You went into the tent then and built a fire in the stove, and during the night used up all the wood except two pieces too long to put in the stove, but you tried to get them in.

"You found some soda crackers in a box, and from the crumbs we guessed it was about half full. Just outside the tent there was a cache of food pulled into a tree to keep it out of the reach of bears. You didn't see that, but you should have heard your horse snorting and jumping around in the corral—an old black bear came around pretty close to the tent.

"You lay down on the ground beside the fire, but if you slept any, it wasn't much. Too many cigarette butts."

During this recitation, every dude in the tent sat with his mouth open and when the guide stopped talking, I glanced at the hunter who had been lost. He held my eye.

"I wonder why I didn't see that fellow," he said. "He must have been right behind me all the time."

Tracks and sign left by any animal, including human, often tell an accurate and fascinating story to the man with the ability to see and then to interpret what he sees.

6 Listening in the Outdoors

MUCH OF the beauty and enchantment of the woods would be lost upon us if we had only eyes to see but no means to hear the sounds of nature—the quiet music of a trout stream, the murmur of wind in a pine forest, the forlorn chirp of a lonely cricket at twilight. Being able to hear the crack of a stick, the inquiring cluck of a gobbler, the roar of wings as a quail covey leaves the ground, the ringing bugle of a bull elk, the splash of bass feeding in the shallows, the gabble of Canada geese in the distance, and myriad other musical sounds, not only adds to your enjoyment of the world beyond the back door steps, but to your hunting and fishing success as well. Often the grunts and growls and squeals and barks and chirps will tell you much about what is happening beyond the limits of your vision. They may prepare you for what you are about to witness, or warn you of impending danger.

It is desirable, therefore, to devote the same attention to training the ear as one gives to the eye, if he wants to develop himself into a top-notch woodsman. This is not too difficult an assignment, for the eye and ear may be trained together by making a conscious effort to listen while we look.

HOW WE HEAR SOUND

As with the eye and sight, the ear is a most amazing assemblage of flesh, bones and fluids, arranged in such a manner that they pick up air waves of certain frequencies and convert them into electrical impulses for transmission to that part of the brain geared to interpret them for pleasure, action or cataloging.

Just how is this done?

The organ for hearing is divided into three parts: the outer, middle and inner ears, all of which have a part in the transmission and translation of sound waves.

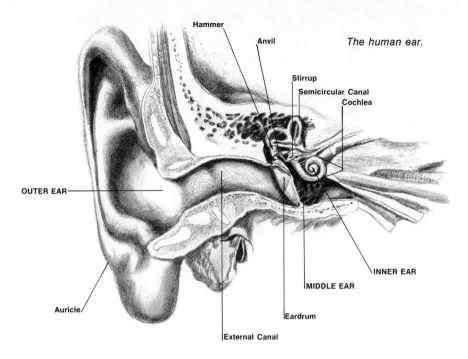

Hammer
Anvil
Stirrup
Semicircular Canal
Cochlea
The human ear.
OUTER EAR
INNER EAR
MIDDLE EAR
Auricle
Eardrum
External Canal

Before you go any farther, pause and take a look at how the top of your ear folds over into a sort of semiflap. This is known as the "helix" and is thought to be a hand-me-down from some of man's ancestors. Human ears in the remote and primitive past were thought to be the "pickup" type, somewhat similar to those of a dog or deer. A few millions of years ago, man's ability to see and hear was a key to his survival, and as that need decreased over thousands of generations, the ability decreased with it and the helix degenerated into a token flap-reminder of those days when our species was young.

To understand how much better than you or I the prick-eared animals can hear, find a quiet spot somewhere and cup a hand behind your ear to listen. You will be amazed at the number of sounds you had not heard before that come into focus. You may pick up the distant call of a crow, the tinkle of a leaf falling through the stillness, the almost inaudible chirp of a bird or insect.

I often use this trick for hunting. It has given me information that I never would have had without it, and has been responsible for my success in bagging at least a few of my trophies.

The outer ear is connected to the middle ear by a tube about an inch long. You can feel it with the end of your finger. The technical term for this tube is "external auditory meatus." Its inner two-thirds is bony and closed on the end by a stretched piece of skin known as the "tympanic membrane." Some of us know it as the eardrum.

Sound waves pouring through this tube hit against the eardrum and cause it to vibrate. This vibration is picked up by the hammer, anvil and stirrup,

To understand how well the prick-eared animals can hear, find a quiet spot somewhere and cup a hand behind your ear to listen.

the three smallest bones in the human body. A special muscle is attached to the eardrum and hammer and acts automatically to adjust these for different sound intensities. This is nature's way of preventing injury—and even rupture—to the delicate membranes when they are bombarded by high-intensity sounds.

The hammer and anvil bones have been termed an "elastic bridge" over which the vibrations are transmitted to the footplate of the stirrup, which presses against the oval window in the inner ear. Oscillations that have reached this window continue on into the fluid-filled canals of the inner ear. These are enclosed in the cochlea, which is spiraled and shaped like a snail shell, from which it gets its name.

A part of the partition dividing the canals is made up of a fibrous, harplike structure called the "basilar membrane." This vibrates under the impact of sound waves passing through the liquid of the upper and lower channels of the cochlea.

On top of this basilar sounding board is the organ of Corti, which might be termed the transformer that converts the waves which come to it through air, skin, bone and liquid into the electrical impulses that reach our brain cells. In the organ of Corti are embedded tiny hair cells responsible for this transformation.

The sound waves from the outside reach the basilar sounding board, causing different parts of it to vibrate in tune to the different frequencies. Separate hair cells of the organ of Corti respond to these frequencies, picking them up as minute electrical charges. These are fed to the auditory nerve fibers and carried on to the brain cells, which break them down and identify them as words spoken, music, or a stick cracking underfoot somewhere ahead of you in the forest.

We can usually judge both the distance and direction of sound. If we are familiar with a certain sound, we can normally guess how close or how far away it is by its degree of loudness. Sometimes, however, the sounds with which we are most familiar will fool us. I have heard quail calling softly to one another from a few yards away and thought they were on the next hillside.

Experiments have been made to determine how the ears can tell direction, and reasonably conclusive proof shows that this human organ is so very sensitive that even from great distances and with the sound waves traveling at an average speed of 1,125 feet per second—depending on the temperature—the ear nearer the origin of the sound picks it up first and also detects a difference in the intensity.

An interesting fact brought out by the experiments is that when the sound comes from directly in front, behind or overhead and strikes both ears of a blindfolded man at the same instant he has no idea of its direction. In such an experiment—or in the woods—this might be remedied by turning the head slightly to one side.

The quickness of the human ear to pick up sounds was verified by having a blindfolded person sit with a telephone receiver over each ear. Two clicks, 1/1000 of a second apart, were fed into the phones. He heard only one click, but always on the side of the receiver that clicked first.

At 2/1000 of a second, the two clicks were identified separately. When the clicks were flashed simultaneously, the sound appeared to be right in front of the tester.

The scale of frequencies the human ear can register runs from 16 to 20,000 cycles per second, and the eardrums are most sensitive to sounds between 1,000 and 5,000 cycles. The normal range of sound for man is about 10½ octaves—the standard piano keyboard covers 7⅓ octaves.

This span of cycles that the ear is able to pick up begins to decrease with age. Some young people have ears quick enough to hear 23,000 cycles. This elasticity of the ear parts changes as we grow older. Few persons over sixty can hear more than 8,000 cycles.

The capability of distinguishing sound extends over a much wider range in both the domestic and wild animals. The life of a wild creature depends on its ears as well as its eyes. Its auditory sense often warns it of danger before it sees it, and in many animals is the means by which they get a meal. Man no longer has such problems.

We know of no tests made on wild animals, but the ears of domestic cats and dogs cover a much wider range than those of their masters. Below 2,000 cycles, these animals hear about the same as man, but sensitivity increases rapidly above the 2,000 mark, and they can distinguish sounds up to 60,000 cycles. The hearing mechanism of the wild members of both tribes is probably sharper.

To point up this difference in sound range, a dog whistle on the market works most effectively on the canine tribe, but is inaudible to human ears.

EXPERIENCES WITH SOUND

As with many other of our physical assets, we never realize how much the ability to distinguish and interpret sounds means to us until our hearing begins

He couldn't hear the quail that thundered off the ground behind us, or off to one side and not in the range of his vision.

to degenerate. Not long ago I hunted quail with a fellow who is deaf enough to need a hearing aid when he is in his office or in business meetings, but must figure that outdoors his ears need no assistance. When we went out after bobwhites together, he left his hearing aid at home.

Neither of us was long in discovering what a mistake that was. My shooting partner got less than one-fourth of the shots he should have had. His only targets that day were the birds that got up right in front of him and that he could see. He could not hear the quail that thundered off the ground behind us, or off to one side and not in the range of his vision. As a result, he missed at least three-fourths of the fun, and although he is a better shot than I, he bagged less than half as many bobs and hens as I was able to put in the game pocket of my hunting coat.

On another occasion I was with an old swamper at daylight in the woods. Spring gobbling season was in and spring itself was bursting with blossom and with song. We leaned against the trunk of a big white oak and watched

dawn seep through the hardwood forest around us. One by one the birds began to stir and soon the morning rang with a cascade of music. I was lost in the melody when the swamper touched my arm.

"Hear that?"

I'm sure he caught the blank expression on my face.

"That old gobbler sounding off. Sure sounds like he's ready for a mite of courting. There he goes ag'in!"

Whatever sound he had heard was lost completely on my duller ears, or in the songbird symphony of the morning.

"Sounds like he's still on the roost," my partner said.

Under such circumstances, a hunter's best bet is to get as close to the gobbler as possible without being seen, conceal himself in a natural blind and start calling. We took off at a fast clip in the direction from which the gobbling had come, and had walked a couple of hundred yards before my ears could pick up the turkey's ringing call.

All the while we were enticing the gobbler in range, and even later, I continued to ruminate over that daylight incident and why the swamper's ears had been able to distinguish those notes where mine had failed. I was a bit younger than the old man and knew that my hearing should have been just as keen, and finally consoled myself with the thought that with his vaster experience he had been more clearly aware of the sound we listened for than had I.

Having perceptive ears is an asset in almost any kind of outdoor endeavor. Especially does it apply to the study of birds, where a chirp or snatch of song out of the brush is often the only clue to the presence of a certain feathered citizen. If you do not recognize the call, you will want to find and identify the songster through your binoculars. If you are familiar with the note, you may want to look over its creator anyway.

In bird study, the training of the ears is as necessary as the development of the eyes. Although we, as humans, have long since lost that section of "pricked-up" ears with which our ancestors were blessed—or cursed—we must learn to keep them pricked up anyway, to record every lisp or warble which might indicate a new species for our records. This conscious effort at listening improves your hearing every time you go into the field, and gives you countless hours of enchantment and gratification.

Bill Rae and I were gobbler hunting with Brooks Holleman at his Turkey Hollow Estate over in Alabama. As far as I know, Bill has never taken up bird watching in the strictest sense of the term, but he is a student of everything outdoors and knows both the song and plumage of a great many birds.

The creek bottoms, swamps and wooded hillsides around the Holleman hunting preserve are one of the most active places I have seen in that part of the spring the cotton state allots to its gobbler hunters. The woods and brush and open meadows are alive with color and song. Curious cardinals and jays perch almost in the blind with you and go through motions which might make you think they have taken up people watching as a hobby. Mocking birds, catbirds and thrashers gather around to serenade you and a never-ending stream of feathered travelers pass on their way to summer homelands. This is an ornithologist's paradise if ever I saw one.

At Turkey Hollow we usually hunted in separate locations every morning, and one day at noon Bill came into camp with such a rapt look in his eyes that I was sure he had bagged the biggest gobbler in Alabama.

"Well, hold him up," I said.

Bill looked blank for an instant, then grinned.

"That gobbler pulled one of his fancy didos and circled around behind us. But we'll get him tomorrow."

He made that statement as though it was relatively unimportant and his eyes lighted up again.

"All morning I've been listening to the most exquisite bird song I've ever heard. It's like a couple of low liquid notes right out of a trout riffle. I couldn't wait to get in and let you tell me what bird it is."

"Did you see it?"

"I never could," he admitted. "It was somewhere up in the branches of a thick tree in front of the blind. It sure stirred up those genes that make me want to go looking for a pair of trout-stream waders."

"Must be a rare species," I said, defending my lack of knowledge. "I don't recognize it from your description, but I'll sure listen."

Now in gobbler hunting anything can happen and usually does. And always when it is least expected. At daylight I had gone to the yodel of an old buck turkey, gotten his attention with my yelper, and after that traded small talk with him until I was sure I had him coming my way. My back was to a sizable beech tree and I was straining both my eyes to catch a movement of leaves, a bright eye or a touch of red wattle to tell me my gobbler was in range.

This was exactly the moment Bill's bird chose to burst into song right over my head. It was a bright little rill, just as my gobbler hunting partner had described it. To save my soul I could not help looking up. I might have stifled the impulse had I known the buck turkey was so near. When my head moved, the gobbler said, "Phutt! Phutt!" and I could hear him moving away through the leaves.

To say that I was irritated with myself would be putting it mildly. But now that my Thanksgiving dinner was well on the way to some other swamp, I swapped my gun for the binoculars and moved to get a better look into the tree overhead. When I got to my feet, the small bird flew off, too, and with the exception of the excitement, I had a vacant morning.

What really amazed me was that after this particular episode I seemed to meet up with those notes almost every time I sat down in one of the swamps or creek bottoms of Turkey Hollow. Yet for some reason I had never heard the song until Bill called it to my attention. It made me realize how many other bird notes I had probably been missing over the many years I have been knocking around in the outdoors. I had been trained in hunting, fishing, bird watching and other such activities, but certainly not all the way.

I eventually did find the bird in my field glasses, and had to look twice to believe what I saw. It turned out to be a cowbird, that free-loading citizen that lays its eggs in the nests of other birds, and thus shirks its family responsibilities. I had watched literally thousands of cowbirds, but for the first time I was conscious of its song.

For me, all of this was another lesson in outdoor observation.

7 Animal Sounds— What They Mean

WILD CREATURES have a language of their own. Each species, in its way, is able to express fear, pleasure, warning and other emotions we often recognize when we become acquainted with the tones and inflections used to indicate them.

Since we are more familiar with the animals we have domesticated as pets or to serve us in many ways, let us first take some of them as examples and show how the voice inflections they use can convey messages to us in such a manner that we understand exactly what they are saying.

Any child knows the difference between the contented purr of a cat and the angry rasp of its voice when it is angry. And who can fail to interpret the caterwauling of an old tom on the backyard fence at two o'clock in the morning when he is in a romantic mood? Your favorite dog will whine when he wants attention, growl a warning when you or I are trespassing on his rights or he thinks you are a threat to something he owns or someone he loves. Who can mistake the eager whinny from the frightened neigh of a horse?

This language we understand from the animals close to us. The same kind of communication exists between the animals, birds and other creatures we catalog as "wild."

I stood with a guide on an open slope above a remote Alaska lake. Between us and the beach where waves lapped against the sand, stood a two-hundred-yard strip of alders and willows, veined with trails padded down by generations of Kodiak bears traveling from one salmon stream to another that fed the lake. He touched my arm when the voice of a bear drifted out of the nearby willows. My hands tightened on my rifle. I was sure we were about to be attacked. My guide merely smiled.

"Something down there caught our scent," he said. "The critter wasn't expressing a thing but curiosity. I think it knows what we are, but not exactly where."

Later I learned the difference between that inquisitive "Woof!" and the angry roar of a charging bear that made the very ground around us tremble. And the second time there was not the slightest uncertainty as to what he meant.

Scientists believe that our first communication with another species may be with the dolphin, known to most of us as the porpoise. This mammal of the sea has a most diversified vocabulary, and has several times been known to duplicate exactly human words that it had heard, though probably this was no more than an attempt at mimicking. They say also that the dolphin's brain cavity is very large, indicating a high degree of intelligence and it may realize that we are trying to establish some degree of understanding. Should we ever be able to find a key or formula to its vocabulary, which would allow us to talk with the dolphin, this may be the breakthrough to hearing many animal sounds as actual words.

BIRD TALK

Most naturalists believe that the common crow has an extensive vocabulary. The longer one associates with this bird, the more one is convinced of this fact. Ernest Thompson Seton, a practical and inquisitive outdoorsman of a generation ago, made an attempt to put the various crow notes to music, with an explanation of what each one meant. He discovered more ways a crow knew how to say "Caw" than one not on intimate terms with the bird would think possible; and each meant something—the sighting of food, a hawk or owl, baby talk to fledglings in the nest, danger, assembly and other messages.

I know one crow word and am as certain of it as if the birds had pronounced it in English. A couple of my farmer friends were having some disagreement with a flock of crows over the final disposition of their watermelon crop. Just before each melon was ripe enough to harvest, the black birds would slip into the field and test its degree of ripeness for themselves, by pecking a plug out of the middle of the melon. The usual scarecrows of old clothes and a hat erected on a pole and crossarm to resemble a man, of white strings stretched across the field, of white paper hung to flap in the breeze, did not work.

The only solution seemed to be to wipe out the flock, so they sent off for a crow call record, put it on a record player and amplifier in a stretch of pines adjoining the watermelon patch, and laid in wait with their scatterguns.

The melon marauders flocked to the call and my friends rid themselves of seven of the enemy before the flock decided it was a victim of deception and retreated. They even stayed away from the melons for a couple of days.

They could not resist the loaded plot for long, however, and when they started their raids again, the farmers called me in to watch the slaughter over their record and amplifier. It made such a racket of crow sounds that ear plugs would have been a relief. We continued to watch beyond the treetops for the circling black horde my friends had promised, but it never materialized. The record ran down and in the almost stunned silence that followed, one old crow somewhere off in the distance answered it with a bored "Aw-caw," and I couldn't have understood the word any better if he had said it in plain English.

I know exactly what a bluejay says when he discovers me wrapped in camouflage from head to toe and hidden—or so I think—in a turkey blind. Almost without fail, this happens when I have caught the attention and interest of a gobbler with my notes of a hen turkey and have reason to suspect that the buck bird is on his way to investigate. The jay has also heard my notes, and being a curious sprite of the woodland, comes over for a look of his own. I hear his wings as he lights in the tree limbs overhead, and do not look up, but intuition tells me he is up there, hopping around in the tree for a better angle, cocking his head sideways to puzzle out my shape.

Finally it dawns on him and he lets out a yell that would wake the ghosts of Bancroft—"A man!!, A man!!!, A man!!!!" The word is as unmistakable as if he had shouted it in English, and every creature within range of his voice knows exactly what he has found. I once located a deer-hunting partner in the woods after two jays told me exactly where he was. That word in jaybirdese could never be misinterpreted for any other.

Magpies have the same obnoxious character trait. One will follow you through the forest or up a ravine, castigating you with every vile word and phrase he knows, and in the meantime warning every other citizen on that particular bit of real estate that you are a threat to life, limb and continued survival. Magpies have discovered me stalking to get into position for a shot, and have cost me some good trophies over the years.

Most woodsmen, however, know that, if properly diagnosed, this abuse can be turned into an asset, for the abusers do not waste their talents on man alone. The presence of any large creature seems to offend them and they will chase after a deer or bear with the same enthusiasm they use on a human. I bagged one of my largest wild gobblers by listening to and understanding this language of the woods.

Turkeys do their lovemaking in the early morning hours. An old gobbler must wake up thinking about sex, for often he will gobble on the roost before he flies down to begin his activities of the day. He hits the ground gobbling, strutting, drumming, talking to the hens and usually keeps this up until mid-morning, after which he seems to lose all interest in the opposite sex and devotes himself to a quest for vittles.

This is the time when most turkey hunters give up the chase and go back to their camps or cars to relax through the day until late afternoon, at which time they seat themselves in some likely spot and listen for the big birds to fly up to roost. Just before dusk the toms will often gobble in answer to the hoot of an owl.

The middle of the day will not be wasted as a turkey hunting period if you know how to use it. Many of the old-timers sit out the midday hours in a blind and are often successful at this. I don't have that brand of patience, so I wander, pause, call, stop, look and listen. What I listen for mostly is a congregation of crows. They will gang up on a turkey almost as quickly as they tackle a hawk or owl.

I had passed through the early morning hours without hearing a gobble and was on my way across a series of low ridges when I heard a flock of crows in the distance. I walked half a mile closer, sat down to listen for a few minutes and was convinced that the crows had found a turkey, and were indulging in the sport of annoying it. They have a special language for turkey worrying.

I approached closer until I could see the crows. They were low in the limbs of trees, taking turns at diving toward the ground and being very vociferous about it all. I could not see the turkey, but knew it was there.

Twenty minutes of watching told me the direction in which the tom was feeding. I backed off, made a wide detour to get in front of the bird, built a makeshift blind, yelped on my turkey call and sat down to wait. I knew the crows heard my yelp because one flew two-thirds of the way over to investigate before his comrades set up a new clamour and he went back to join the fun. If the crows heard it, the gobbler had heard it too, and it was only natural that he would feed in the direction of another turkey.

It was as I had guessed. After a while the crows tired of their sport and flew off to find a new diversion, and a long time later I heard scratching in the leaves just over the contour of the hill in front of me. To establish my location a last time, I clucked, put the gun to my shoulder in a comfortable position with my elbows on my knees and waited.

At my cluck, the scratching stopped for a minute, then resumed as the bird continued feeding. But I was in no hurry. I knew he'd eventually get there. He fed on up the slope, almost casually, and not more than twenty yards away put his head up to look around.

It was as simple as that. This was one gobbler I bagged in which a series of different sounds that I was able to interpret played the most important role.

The language of the smaller birds is a varied one. They use certain notes when they are announcing to the world that this is their home territory and they intend to tolerate no trespassing. We call this singing and marvel at its sweetness of melody, but making music is not exactly what they have in mind. They use other notes when they are feeding their young, and still others when a predator wanders by. You can be sure that something important is happening in the avian world when a group of the songsters get together and fill the woods with excited chirps. The more successful outdoorsman—hunter, hiker or student of birds—notes these sounds. They mean something to him.

SQUIRRELS

The squirrels have a language of their own and they don't hesitate to use it. You can learn a lot of words in squirrelese by slipping as slowly and quietly as possible through the woods, pausing frequently and for long periods until you manage to let a squirrel discover you. Stop there and listen to him carefully. If he thinks you are an intruder only and that he is relatively out of danger, he'll talk one way: his degree of annoyance will to some extent govern his conversation. There is a great difference in the way he barks when he hangs head down on a tree trunk and merely suggests that you go elsewhere, and his chatter of alarm, accompanied by the rattle of bark, when one of the fast hawks swings into his stretch of woods, or a pine martin appears anywhere around him.

I had an opportunity to note that difference when I was pussyfooting through a spruce forest high in the Rocky Mountains. The carpet of needles was wet and by taking one slow step at a time and watching where I set down each foot to keep from breaking a twig or stick, I was traveling about as quietly as it was possible for me to move through the timber. The high valley was loaded with elk sign and I was hoping to come upon an outsized bull, standing with its muzzle into the air currents and taking its noonday siesta.

Naturally there is no way of knowing how many unseen eyes watch as you pick your way through a stretch of woods, and never betray their presence. When a red squirrel set up a chattering several trees ahead, I gathered from his tone and from the fact that he had been otherwise occupied until I was almost under him, that I, and not an elk or other animal, was the cause of his excitement.

I paused, studying the trees ahead until I located the squirrel and discovered that he did have his attention beamed on me. Under such a circumstance, when you are on a stalk, you can do one of two things—either move on ahead and out of range of his voice, or stop dead still until he loses interest in you. I chose the latter and continued to watch the little creature, whose diminishing chatter indicated that he was beginning to accept me as a part of his community, when all of a sudden his tone changed drastically. This could mean only one thing: someone else was with us in that stretch of timber.

I searched the forest floor ahead in minute detail. I ruled out another human. It could not have been one of the hoofed animals or even a bear, for the squirrel was too frantic. Then my eye picked up a movement beyond the base of the spruce tree occupied by the squirrel, and two pine martens slid into view around the end of an old log. They appeared interested in some private matter and for a few moments showed not the slightest concern for the red squirrel in the treetop above them. Then one of the martens—and I am sure this was deliberate devilment and nothing else—calmly moved over to the base of the spruce occupied by the squirrel, stood on its hind legs and put its paws on the tree as though it had climbing in mind. The squirrel screeched once, the bark rattled and a few flakes came drifting down through the crowns. The little brown fellow simply shut up and disappeared. The marten stood another minute, looking up, then joined his companion and they moved out of sight into the timber.

This is one of only three times that I have ever seen pine martens in the wild, but it left me with an impressive lesson in the language of the forest.

Then my eye picked up a movement beyond the base of the spruce tree occupied by the squirrel, and two pine martens slid into view.

DEVELOPING A SENSITIVE EAR

Just how would you and I go about learning the myriad wild words, tones, rustlings, rattlings and other noises in the outdoors? No one has ever devised a formula for this and proficiency doesn't come overnight. But the acquisition of this ability can give you some of your most pleasant experiences in the outdoors.

You can increase the sensitivity of your ear to all wilderness sounds by consciously forcing yourself to hear and record every sound until this attention becomes almost second nature. This does not mean that you can compel your ears to hear 40,000 cycles where you now hear only 14,000, but you can learn to distinguish those sounds which do come within the scope and limits of your auditory senses.

There are several ways to begin this. An ornithologist, when he wants to observe a certain bird, or to determine the number of species or individuals in an area, wets the skin on the back of his hand with his lips and sucks against the skin to make a squeaking sound similar to that made by a mouse in trouble. Usually every creature within sound of the squeak will come over to investigate it. Most are merely curious; some anticipate a meal. Birds you would never suspect are there. They pop out of the bushes and swing on a nearby limb, chirping excitedly, and it does not take long to gather a crowd.

Often your audience will include other creatures, too. Once I was partially hidden by a log in a thicket that my squeaking had brought alive with birds. My ears caught a rustling on the other side of the log and I raised myself slowly to peep over and identify the sound. At a level with the top of the log, I found myself eye to eye with a big black snake that had come to find the mouse in trouble. I've also been stalked by hawks and foxes.

This squeaking is also a good way to see a bird you can hear but cannot find with your eyes. Many bird songs are ethereal in quality, with a ventriloquil echo which makes them seem to come from one place one instant and from an entirely different place the next. The squeaking will often bring such an elusive individual out of hiding.

One of the most interesting ways I know to help improve your sound perception is to occasionally take an afternoon off for just listening in the woods. Use your eyes as much as you like, but concentrate especially on what those delicate parts of your auditory organ can pick up.

When you first move into a stretch of woods and sit down, everything around you will be as still as death. Every creature within sight and hearing knows you are there. As a precaution, they stop feeding, and stirring and singing, sometimes for as long as a quarter of an hour before they accept your presence and get back to normal activity, and the forest again comes to life.

Carry along a note pad to make notes, if you like, of every different sound you hear. Pick a day when there is no wind or rain and the trees are at rest. Don't stop too close to the brawling voice of a stream. Sit still and listen. You may be surprised at how long your list of sounds will be, and at some of the items on it: a falling leaf, bumping softly or rattling down through the other leaves and branches; the silken whistle of a dove's wing feathers as it takes off or alights; the "flap-flap-flap, flap-flap-flap" of a woodpecker on its erratic flight pattern; the roar of a quail as it wings off the ground, the swish of teal wings overhead and the slower beat of mallards; the low drone of a humming bird. The wings of almost every kind of bird make a different and identifiable sound when in flight, even though you may have difficulty in identifying some of the smaller species by their wing beats, or even hearing them in flight.

You will probably recognize the rattle of bark from a squirrel on a tree trunk—there is no other sound quite like that—or a towhee scratching in the leaves of the forest floor, the snort of a deer, the whine of an investigating mosquito or bee, the chirp of a tree frog, and dozens of other noises. Many you will be able to identify, but you will need the help of your eyes to recognize others.

Once I associated for a while with a fellow who had spent his life on a quiet, backwoods southern river, and as far as I knew, he never missed a sight or sound. He recognized the sound of a snake dropping off a tree limb into the water, a turtle sliding off a log, a kingfisher diving for its food, a frog jumping off the bank, a duck getting off the surface. Each and every one was as clear to him as a spoken word.

Only once did I see him baffled. We were gliding silently along in his boat to reach a favorite fishing bank when something around the next bend splashed the surface of the river. He stopped paddling to listen and it came again. I looked back and his eyes met mine, but we did not speak. He put his paddle quietly into the water and we slid around the curve. Two youngsters were there, from a farmhouse just beyond the swamp, amusing themselves by tossing rocks and pieces of rotten limbs into the stream. The riverman grinned at me but made no comment, and I knew he had added another type of splash to those already filed in his memory.

I am certain no one has ever tried to list every sound he recognizes in the outdoors. For a woodsman, the number would run into astronomical figures. The rest of us are constantly adding to our knowledge on this score, with a sense of pleasure in identifying each new rustle, rattle, chirp, or squeak.

One of the ways I have found to train this particular sense is with a tape recorder. After I have been in a spot long enough for the creatures to begin to stir around me, I turn the recorder on and forget it. While it is recording, I try to make a list of every note I hear. Later I compare the tape and notebook and am often surprised that while I was busy concentrating on one sound, the recorder was picking up others that I overlooked.

How many different bird songs can you hear at once, just after daylight on a fine morning in the shank of spring? I was sure that I did not miss a note until I put my tape recorder on the job and tried to out-listen it.

I listed each and every one of those songsters contributing its bit of music to the morning: a cardinal down by the creek and another on the hill; a wren out by the garden; pine warblers in a clump of loblollies on the lawn; a bobwhite sounding off beyond the fence and answered by three more in the distance; a downy woodpecker; an orchard oriole; a catbird; a tufted titmouse; a robin; a whitebreasted nuthatch; a chipping sparrow. I was sure I had them all until I played back my tape in the quiet of my study. Almost drowning out the melody at one point were the raucous notes of a flock of crows passing overhead and I had not even heard them!

This was most humiliating and proved at least one thing—that my ears were probably overlooking a lot of sounds they should have been hearing, and most obvious sounds at that. Also, that no matter how expert a fellow might think he is in this department, the odds are that he still has a long way to go.

8　The Sense of Smell

GEORGE DALTON and I had tied our horses and were slipping along afoot, upwind through a pocket of timber high in the Absaroka Range of Wyoming's Rocky Mountains. The forest floor was spongy and wet, and since we were stepping slowly and carefully enough to avoid sticks or twigs which might snap under our feet, we were drifting along about as soundlessly as a man can move through the forest.

The pocket was full of fresh elk sign. The light air current that stirred was in our faces and there was slight chance of any creature ahead catching our scent. I knew how much better the wild eyes were than ours, and to try to compensate for this, I kept my binoculars in my hand and every few steps paused to use them and sweep the forest for any horizontal line, patch of color, or movement that might give away the presence of an elk.

Even with all this precaution, the first indication we had of bulls and cows was a very strong odor brought to us down the air currents. George and I both got it about the same time and he paused in the act of raising a foot to take a step. Very slowly I lifted my glasses to study every forest aisle and shadow in the direction from which the scent had come. While I watched, we heard a dead tree limb break with a sharp crack. George and I traded glances. We knew that in spite of our precautions, the sharp eyes of an animal had seen us first.

We walked on slowly, continuing to glass ahead, and found a small grassy meadow with a bright little stream winding through it. Fresh sign was all over the place, the smell of elk hung in the air, and tracks showed where the herd had vacated its hideout and spooked in the direction of a tremendous wooded canyon just beyond the ridge. I sniffed around the place like a curious hound and located the strongest scent spot, where the herd bull had urinated on his hocks, which apparently is one of the rituals at mating time. The ground was still wet.

This was not the first time I had located elk by smell. Dick Loftsgarten of the T E Ranch and I were scouting around in a strip of forest close up against timberline, looking for a bull we had glassed earlier in the day. I was ahead, just inside a line of trees, when the smell of the herd came so strongly that I knew it must be close. Dick was inches behind me when we spotted the elk, spaced out in the timber. The animals appeared to be taking a noonday siesta, and we stood there long enough to look them over. Try as we might, we could not get a glimpse of the big-antlered bull we had watched from a parallel ridge earlier in the day.

I turned to ask in a whisper whether we should look further for the trophy bull, or take a spike we could see off to our right in the timber, and a stick underfoot broke as I shifted my weight. At least a dozen animals were in the herd and they moved as one, crashing off through the woods with as much commotion as a herd of stampeding elephants.

"You'd sure have had to make your mind up in a hurry after you broke that stick," Dick laughed.

Another time Anson Eddy and I were afoot on the high ridge that leads down to Hawk's Rest Mountain above Bridger Lake in the Thorofare. We got a whiff of the bull long before we saw it and crawled on our hands and knees along a side hill leading into a low pass. The scent of the bull remained strong, but to save our souls we could not seem to locate it. At Anson's suggestion, I slid forward to an old log and raised myself high enough to look over the hillside contour just ahead. The bull was there, his head turned back over his shoulder in our direction, not more than seventy-five yards away.

I am sure he saw my head when I put it above the rim of the log and was probably trying to decide what manner of critter I might be. He stood for the fraction of a minute I needed to slowly pull my rifle into position and I felled him with a neck shot.

My experience is that some persons have a better sense of smell than others. Almost anyone can detect the temper of a displeased skunk or the billy goat essence a big rattlesnake exudes when it feels the urge to warn away intruders. The smells of coffee or bacon cooking over a campfire will often roll us out of the sleeping bag sooner than we intended to hit the cold morning air. Almost any fisherman can stick his nose into the scent trail of a bream bed and trail it to a shallow point or into a cove. Yet I have been in a boat with anglers who argued that no such perception existed, and who could not catch the sardiny fragrance of bream when we sat squarely on top of an acre of beds.

A few times I have caught the unmistakable musk of a whitetail buck, even before I saw him step into sight around the bend of a game trail. A number of southern mountaineers I know excel in this respect. I used to consider that Wade Patterson, who spent his life in the Blue Ridge, was pulling my shin bone when he would stop on a mountain trail, put his nose up and say, "Thar's a deer been along here."

Then one day, on a muddy section of the trail, just after he had made such an announcement, we found the big track of a whitetail buck and it could not have been more than minutes old. I never doubted him after that.

Deer must give off a very strong and exciting scent, because every dog I have ever met loves to run one. This includes the well-bred and well-behaved pointers, which obey every command that has to do with quail, but which cannot resist taking off after a deer. To have such a large animal flee in front of him must give a dog a most superior complex.

I was quail hunting in south Georgia with one of the finest covey and single-bird pointers I have seen. He knew his business and was giving us some mighty fine covey rises and singles shooting, too, until we jumped a small buck out of a thicket. The pointer took off behind it in full voice that would have been a credit to a Plott hound. His owner whistled and yelled at him until he went out of sight, then sadly shook his head.

"I won't see him again until tomorrow. And if I'm as mad at him then as I am now, I'll cut off his tail right behind his ears, sure as sin."

I've often thought how much more pleasure the woods would be if a fellow's sense of smell was as efficient as that of a dog and he could scent-read what goes on within range of his nose, or what has already happened there. I am sure that such highly developed olfactory nerves would greatly increase his enjoyment of the outdoors, as well as his hunting success, by preparing him in advance and possibly restrain him from blundering along in such a manner as to put animals and other creatures on the alert.

Over many millenniums man gradually threw the burden of his existence on his eyes and ears, while his sense of smell slowly deteriorated. Fortunately, our olfactory organ remains powerful enough so that we continue to depend on it in many ways. One of the most important of those is taste, the substance of which is largely smell. The combination of these two senses helps us to relish food and often warns us when meats and vegetables and such are tainted or otherwise unfit for human consumption.

Our noses help us to enjoy the outdoors, by taking in the delightful perfumes of flowers, the tangy sweetness of the pines, the fragrance of a forested glade with its humus and rotting wood and tree leaves of many kinds, each with an odor of its own.

One of my old friends and a top outdoor writer of his time, Elmer Ransom, used to say, "I love the rich, ripe smell of marshland when the tide is out." The seashore beaches, and the dunes and marsh behind them, with their thousand odors, would never be as intriguing were we unable to enjoy them by scent as well as by sight and sound.

No one can say for certain how highly developed the first humans' sense of smell might have been. The odds are that this was one of the faculties that helped them locate edible plants, and it was probably strong enough to detect edible birds and animals, and warn them of predatory animals.

We do know that some primitive tribes have a more highly developed sense of smell than city dwellers. Our noses are deadened by constant contact with such things as tobacco, carbon gases, dust and smoke of many varieties. Often I find that when I have been in the woods for a month or more, away from the frightful smells of civilization, my sense of smell becomes much keener than normal.

I have never met up with a native who could trail an animal by scent, but some of my gunning partners have, when they were off in other parts of the world. A frightened or wounded animal is said to give off a stronger odor, and this may be true. We do know that under certain circumstances, the adrenal gland releases adrenaline into the bloodstream, which apparently creates some kind of odor, for dogs and other creatures with extraordinary smell instantly sense when a human is afraid.

Even though we are unable to perform such stunts as pointing a covey of quail, or sniffing out a rabbit in its bed, we humans are not so limited as to be totally unaware of odors. Just how we capture and translate these odors is an interesting phenomenon.

In nature there is no such thing as completely pure, unadulterated air. Creatures, plants and other matter give off chemicals which are soaked up by the element we call air. These chemicals and combinations of chemicals are held in suspension and carried along on the wings of the wind until they are dissipated.

Most of the air we breathe goes down our windpipe into the lungs. From this current of air that carries oxygen to the lung tissues, eddies circulate through the upper passageways of the nose and come in contact with a cellular, membrane-like tissue in the very roof of the nose. The thin, syrupy mucus covering this membrane absorbs the chemicals in the air. The sensations created by the various chemicals are picked up by microscopic hairs on the end of long, thin cells called olfactory receptors, which extend from this tissue up into the olfactory bulb of the brain.

Each of these receptor cells is thought to behave differently in its reaction to one kind or another of the basic smell chemicals. In the olfactory bulb, these degrees of stimulation are converted into electrical impulses which are fed into a highly complicated network of neurons, or nerve fibers, and fed on to the frontal lobe of the brain, which identifies a particular odor or combination of odors.

Animals with a highly developed sense of smell have a larger portion of the forebrain devoted to this function than those without this ability. A rat, which is known for its exceptionally keen nose, has a much greater percentage of its forebrain devoted to capturing and identifying odors than do man and many of the other animals. It finds most of its food by smelling. We have other ways of getting enough to eat.

The combination of mucus, cell receptors and nerve fibers warns us when food is spoiled, whether there is a gas leak in the house, not to drink certain liquids such as gasoline and household ammonia. With some exceptions, outdoor odors are usually not as strong as many of those created by man, but even with this fainter fragrance, our noses give us the same pleasant sensations, or warn us of situations we cannot see or hear.

In at least a few experiences over many years, I have found myself in circumstances which produced the strange sensation that I had been in the very same spot and under the same circumstances before, and that what was happening at the moment was an exact repetition of a past occurrence.

Some psychologists say that this may happen when a man's brain is weary and one side is working an infinitesimal fraction of a second faster than the other side. Others, more romantic, think that this may be a throwback to man's primordial past, and that inherited instinct may be responsible for the sensation.

Either way, two such adventures I remember were activated through the sense of smell. One was on an Alaska creek. When I got the strong odor of a bear, I knew it was close, even though I could not see or hear it. That gets your fluids to percolating as nothing else will, and in this instance I felt that mysterious sense of having been there before. Instinctively, I acted just as I imagine one of my cave-days ancestors might have: I simply stood without moving a muscle except those in my eyes, and ready for any action I might have to make in a hurry. Grass and other vegetation around me was higher than my head and I never did see the bear, but a long time after the smell went away I cautiously explored and discovered that I had been frighteningly close to a well-padded bear trail that followed a creek where the salmon ran. The tracks there were wet and very large, indicating that a tremendous Alaska brownie had been in the creek somewhere below our near rendezvous. The wind was such that when he padded by, the bruin was no doubt unaware of my presence, which in those close quarters was unquestionably a most fortunate state of affairs for either him or me—I am pleased that we did not have to find out which.

Another time I spent over a month in the Bahama Islands, breathing the clean, briny air, and I am sure that this improved the functioning of my olfactory organ. Near the end of the trip we made a hunt for wild boars on Great Abaco Island. These were tremendous brutes. They were said to be the progeny of wild pigs introduced some centuries ago by the pirates who preyed on the Spanish Main ships, as a source of fresh meat. Over many generations on the limestone island, the pigs had developed large frames to carry their meat, and tremendous tushes.

We had a couple of races with the smaller animals and along about the middle of the afternoon, our two dogs jumped a boar and carried it at a pell-mell pace into one of the most rugged jungles you can imagine, of limestone slabs and chunks covered with moss, of a thick understory of ferns and brush growing profusely everywhere, and a network of vines reaching up into the larger trees.

Somewhere ahead the dogs bayed. With the camera in my hand, I ran toward the sound, but it was like an obstacle race. The moss-covered limestone made the footing most uncertain and time and again the hidden rocks tripped and threw me. Fortunately the brush and vines were so dense and interwoven that when I fell it was against a wall of vegetation and I never went completely down.

I could smell the boar even before I got to the scene of the fracas. The odor permeated the narrow glade. Without a sight or sound to guide me, I am sure I could have found that pig in the dark.

I crawled in to get a picture of the boar at bay, snapped a flash bulb in the face of the animal, and the boar broke past the two dogs and charged directly at me. The odor of musk was terrific and I am not certain but that I added some fragrance of my own.

For at least a fraction of a second, the thought flashed that I was reliving a drama from some other place and some other time.

Our guide, a native hunter with powerful arms and shoulders, jumped to my rescue with his machete, knocked the pig down with a head blow that stunned it, fell on top of the animal and wrestled it to the ground while I made my escape.

The boar weighed close to 200 pounds, but what struck me at the moment, even more than its size and our near encounter, was my momentary flashback and a belief that had I been able to maintain a fast enough pace through that jungle I could have trailed the animal with my own nose.

The boar broke past the two dogs and charged directly at me.

Your sense of smell can keep you out of trouble in more ways than one. Once I was turned around in a big southern swamp. I knew the region quite well and did not bother to carry my compass when I left camp by starlight for the morning hunt. Shortly after daylight, a buttermilk fog moved in, and almost before I realized it I had not the slightest idea of my direction from camp. I came upon sloughs I am certain I would have recognized under normal conditions of lighting, but they were entirely unfamiliar in the soupy light.

I had planned to get back to camp by mid-morning for breakfast and did not even have a match with me. There wasn't much need to try to hunt—I couldn't see over seventy-five feet. The morning was too uncomfortable to sit and wait for the fog to clear, so I continued to wander, watching for tracks and otherwise making a feeble pretense of hunting.

I was disgusted with myself for getting into a situation such as this and am certain I would have spent a most miserable day—and night, too, for the fog was a two-day affair—had I not suddenly caught the fragrant smell of woodsmoke. At the moment it was one of the sweetest aromas I had ever smelled. I was not long in following it to camp, where I found my partner, who did have the forethought to carry his compass, with the coffeepot and frying pan ready for business.

For the simple novelty of it, try an experiment the next time you are outdoors. On a deer stand, in a duck blind, when you pause to rest beside the trail, close your eyes and sit quietly for a few minutes and test the air currents with your nose. You may or may not be able to recognize any odor, but if you do, it will please you greatly. Also, while you are moving through the woods and fields—whatever the reason—make a point of testing familiar objects with your nose. Break open a mushroom, crush a ripe persimmon in your fingers, twist a minty sliver of birch bark, scrape the lichens off a wet rock, try any number of plants for sweetness or sourness of odor. Some, like the black walnut, mint leaves, pine needles, cherry tree leaves, violets, are already familiar to you. You may find that sniffing around the woods is a most delightful way to pass an afternoon.

9 The Sixth Sense

I WAS ON MY way down a little creek tucked away in one of the remote regions of the southern Appalachian Mountains and bumped smack into an old fishing buddy of mine. I had not seen Roy Ozmer since we talked about these back-country trout waters a couple of years before, so we lit our pipes and sat down on a streamside boulder for a visit and a hearty chuckle that we should happen to land there at the same time. Roy had packed in a light tent fly and grub for three days. He said the fishing was every bit as good as we had guessed it would be.

"I did have one sort of unusual experience," he mused, "that in all my wilderness years, never happened to me before. I've been thinking it over most of the day, trying to figure it out."

He told me about it. He had cleared out a few sprigs of brush and set up his tarp where a small spring branch flowed into the main creek. He collected a pile of firewood, built a fire, cooked a couple of trout he had saved for supper and then settled back with his pipe to enjoy the campfire.

"I don't even remember what I was thinking about," he said. "Nothing in particular, I guess. The fire had burned down to a bed of coals and a few flickers, and I was beginning to get that deliciously tired and relaxed feeling that comes along about bedtime when you are in the woods, and all of a sudden I got a strange, prickly sensation, so strong that it ran over my body like a mild electric shock. I now know what it means when they say a fellow's hair stands on end. I am certain that those on the back of my neck did.

"There was no sound, no movement, nothing except that weird feeling that brought me wide awake, tense and alert for anything that might happen.

"It could not have lasted more than a few seconds, but seemed like minutes before it passed. One thing for sure—I wasn't sleepy anymore. I threw more wood on the fire, relit my pipe and sat there for a long time, trying to put the pieces of the puzzle together."

The next morning after he had built up his fire, put coffee water on and washed his face in the cold creek water, Roy looked around. His mystery of the night before was explained when he found the tracks of a large bobcat on the muddy edge just above the waterline across the creek, not more than forty feet from his campfire.

"What I felt," he said, "could not have come from any other source than those eyes on me. I was conscious of no sound, no movment, no smell. I can just imagine that a few hundreds or thousands of generations ago, some cave-man ancestor of mine had that same feeling when one of the big cats stared at him out of the darkness. His sixth sense, or whatever you choose to call it, warned him of danger, and maybe saved his life."

We do know that man is linked to his evolutionary past, and that some of his behavior today has its roots in the dawn of mankind on this earth. But over many millenniums, the pattern of man's life has become so stereotyped, with his physical being so dependent on food and other material substances produced commercially and plentifully, and his safety from the larger animals practically guaranteed, that all of his senses have dulled.

We have no way of knowing how much stronger the sixth sense was in primitive man. The chances are that this sense, like our other five, has grad-ually deteriorated as man has had less and less occasion to use it.

Although it is rudimentary in today's human, it has not been erased alto-gether, as Roy Ozmer's experience showed. Everyone has it to a certain degree. In a crowd, did you ever look up and find someone's eyes on you? Or have you sat studying some person and had him turn and stare directly at you, as though he could feel your eyes or the wavelengths of your thought? Of course you have had both experiences.

Any experienced woodsman is familiar with all the sounds and noises in the particular bailiwick where he hunts and fishes. When he lies down to sleep beside his campfire, one part of his mind remains alert. It interprets such sounds as wind moving through the trees, the distant call of an owl, a raccoon yodeling its way down the swamp, the bark of a coyote, the musical notes of a whippoorwill or other songster of the darkness. The mind accepts them as normal and its relaxation is in no way disturbed. But just let a stick snap somewhere out there in the night and the woodsman is wide awake in a split second, with all of his faculties alert to identify that sound which does not belong.

I am certain that this sixth sense once save my life. This was long ago when I was a college student who managed to scrape together enough nickles and dimes to spend at least a part of the summer and fall in the Rocky Moun-tains. I worked at outdoor jobs and made enough money to get home again. Most of those jobs were so far back in the wilderness that through the entire summer I seldom saw another human except those working with me in a crew.

Some of the younger members of a trail-building outfit of which I was a part—especially those of us who were avid fans of western story magazines— wore six-shooters when we were in the woods. Who we were trying to pattern ourselves after, I have no idea, but I packed an old stag-handled .32/20 pistol. It came as near anything I ever owned, to getting me in trouble. The occasion was when I made a trip afoot and alone into a mountain range to check on a forest fire which had supposedly been put out but continued to send up smoke.

Late in the afternoon I was walking along a small brushy ridge when a movement ahead caught my eye. By crouching, I could make out a black bear pawing for grubs at the remains of a rotten log. He wasn't more than forty yards away, and was unaware of my presence. Feeling like a Daniel Boone, I unsheathed my revolver, sat down and took a bead on the animal. I don't have to explain how foolish and inexperienced I was to be taking on a bear with a .32/20 pistol bullet.

As luck would have it, I missed just enough for the bullet to plow into and smash the black's spinal column and cord and put him down. I got close enough to get another load into his head and then was surprised to see that, stretched out on the ground, the bear did not seem as large as it had appeared in life. Even so, my shirt buttons were popping off with the pride of my accomplishment.

I dismissed the forest fire temporarily from my mind, figuring that I could tend to that in the morning, pulled the bear over to a tangle of wind-thrown trees and built a fire. I skinned out the bear, cut a chunk of meat off a loin and put it on a stick over the fire. I really was living it up!

I spread the skin out over a log behind the campfire, made coffee and had myself a roast bear dinner that at the time I was sure tasted as good as anything I ever ate.

With the darkness all around me and the campfire burning brightly, I loaded and lit the briar and sat back to glow in the content of my self-satisfaction. But something was missing or wrong, and I could not quite put my mental finger on it. I was neither contented nor comfortable. After a couple of pipefuls of tobacco, I finally decided that my trouble was fatigue. I'd had a long day and nothing was wrong that a good night's sleep would not cure.

I spread out the blanket in my packsack, folded it over me and went to sleep with the campfire flames making a weird pattern of black and gold on the trees.

I have no idea how long I slept, but I was suddenly very wide awake. The campfire had burned to a bed of coals, except for a couple of sticks that threw up flickers of light. I knew just as well as if I had been awake moments before that I had heard a stick break out in the darkness. It could have been a deer, elk or moose, but that sixth sense had a full head of steam going by now and I knew exactly what had made that noise. When I sat up and threw off that blanket, I did not need the low growl I heard beyond the bed of coals to convince me how right I had been.

Moving slowly, I backed around the golden campfire mound with its two barely flickering sticks, with my gun in one hand, straining to see beyond the black wall close around me. I felt for campfire wood with the other hand and fed small, dry pieces to the heap of coals. When they flared up, I imagine my sigh of relief was loud enough to sound like a snort. Another growl, farther out this time, told me that my visitor was moving back from the light. I kept putting on wood until I had a blaze the size of a college bonfire, and was thankful for the supply in the windfall behind me.

Some time after midnight my intruder went away, and I was able to get snatches of sleep until daylight, but did not allow that fire to burn down again.

The next morning I made a thorough search around the place, but I could find no evidence of my visitor. Later, some of the older foresters with whom I was working helped me figure out what had happened. The black bear I had killed with my pistol was a very large two-year-old cub. Cubs rarely stay with their mothers past this age. I had not seen the mother, but she was somewhere nearby when I shot, and she slipped away from the scene without showing herself. She could smell the skin of her cub at the campfire and had returned under the cover of darkness, getting closer as the fire died down. My sixth sense had warned me that she was out there, even before I rolled up in my blanket, though I had not heard a sound. When she moved in close and broke the stick or limb, the remarkable sixth sense told me exactly what I was up against.

Even though you are asleep, part of your mind keeps you informed, and moves you to activity only when the need or reason to act is imperative. It might ignore a situation under certain conditions, and get you going in the same situation when the conditions are different.

Sometimes in the summer I take two- or three-day trips up a back-country trout stream, spending the night where darkness finds me on the stream. I pack along a light load of dried foods, coffee, plastic cups, boiler, flashlight, a small ax, rain gear and a lightweight plastic tarp that can quickly be strung on a rope stretched between two trees for a dry camp, should I run into rainy weather.

Some years ago, a partner and I were sound asleep on a narrow flat bench, slightly above the level of the creek. We cooked our evening meal and went to sleep under a sky studded with stars. Shortly after midnight, I sat up and listened, wondering what had wakened me. A faint flash of light to the east and a minute or two later the distant rumble of thunder, only faintly discernible above the roar of the nearby trout stream, told me that my perception had picked up that first faint echo with the message that something should be done about it. When I moved to get up, my partner stirred.

"What's up?"

"We may or may not be in for a wetting," I said.

Our equipment was scattered around the little bench, with waders, cups, packsacks and other gear spread out on the rocks and logs. We were only minutes in stretching a rope about five feet high between two trees, throwing our plastic tarp over it and pegging it at four corners. Minutes more were required to gouge a shallow trench in the soft earth around the upper side of the shelter, and move all gear, plus a supply of dry wood for the breakfast fire, under the tarp.

The rainstorm passed over us about half an hour later, and even with its thundering and rumbling and beating against our tarp, I was barely conscious of it, so snug and secure were we under the makeshift tent.

I contrasted this experience with one almost a month later when I was quartered in a mountain cabin, and slept through a heavy lightning and rain storm without knowing it until the following morning.

I have talked with any number of fellows who are parttime outdoorsmen with plenty of experience and who live in town. Almost without exception, they say that no matter how many different noises they hear, they are not disturbed except by the unusual. The roar of traffic, a clock striking, a plane overhead, the milkman on his early rounds—those are expected and accepted. But just let a door creak, or a stealthy footstep sound in the driveway, and they are instantly awake.

Amazingly enough, almost every one of those fellows can awaken on a given hour without the aid of an alarm clock, or if the alarm is set, they wake up a minute or two before it goes off.

What makes a fellow walking in the woods suddenly stop for no apparent reason and start looking around him? I have done it at least a hundred times and stood there from one to three or four minutes before I made out a copperhead, black snake, rattler or other snake camouflaged so perfectly in the leaves that it was all but invisible. It would be lying absolutely motionless and none of my other senses perceived it, yet that strange intuition warned me of danger.

Such a feeling overpowered, and I am sure saved, me one night in Wyoming. Dick Loftsgarten and I had been on an all-day elk hunt that ended late in the afternoon at the headwaters of Hoodoo Creek, with a mammoth ridge between us and the ranch. It should have ended there for the day when we found a cabin with an emergency supply of rations and plenty of wood. We decided, however, that by following the Hoodoo Creek trail, we could be back at the ranch some time between sundown and midnight.

Shortly after dark the sky was scudded over with clouds, and when the last vestige of light disappeared in the west, we were riding in the blackest night I ever encountered. We knew the trail skirted a few sheer canyons, so we stayed in the saddle because horses can see very well in the blackest night. In fact, I could hardly make out the shape of my horse's head from a few feet away.

We rode for what seemed like an interminable period, and from the angle of the saddle under me and my weight in it, the trail seemed to level out a bit, though I could not see the ground.

We rode on for another long time and suddenly both horses stopped stock still. I tried to urge my mount forward, then kicked it in the ribs, but the animal would not budge.

"What's going on?" Dick asked from behind me.

"This crazy horse has quit on us," I said. "Maybe I can lead him."

I stepped out of the saddle, feeling with my feet for the ground. I walked around in front of the horse and then stopped. I could not see three feet in that blackness, but I knew just as well as I knew I was standing there that disaster lay very near. The feeling was so strong that it tingled at the base of my scalp.

Feeling in my pocket, I found a packet of paper matches. I struck one and could see nothing but blackness in front of where I stood. I struck another and threw it ahead and as it went out of sight, it burned just long enough to let me know that I stood on the rim of a sheer precipice. One more step would have sent me catapulting into pitch-dark depths that could have been from a dozen to a thousand feet to the bottom.

I retreated slowly and my horse seemed very inclined to back up with me. Once I figured I was on safe ground again, I climbed into the saddle.

"What do we do now?" I asked.

"Swing him to the right and give him his head," Dick replied.

We started off again, with me as tight as a bongo drum, but somehow the horse found his way around whatever we had encountered. About eleven o'clock the moon came up, and even through the clouds it gave us a little light and we rode into the ranch after midnight.

This sixth sense must certainly be inherent, and as far as I know, no way has ever been found to develop it. But from the stories I have heard, and from my own experiences, it is one of our vital perceptions in the outdoors.

10 Patience Can Pay Off

ONE OF THE most important traits anyone can possess to qualify as a competent observer in the outdoors is patience. That is as necessary as a sharp eye and a keen ear. The inability to control the nervous impulse to move has cost many an outdoorsman a trophy.

I am sure that many gunners, anglers, bird students, photographers and naturalists have missed unforgettable moments simply because they lacked perseverance. I can think of dozens of instances when I was successful by staying put just one minute more, and hundreds of other times when I moved or stood up a minute or fraction thereof too soon.

One of the first lessons I ever got in patience was on a trout stream. It was also one of my most valuable bits of education in trout fishing.

Bradley Scott was one of those accomplished artists with a flyrod. He was almost twice my age when we started wading streams together and we caught trout in a dozen states from Georgia to Maine. From his store of knowledge about flyfishing, I learned many lessons that might have been years coming with my own experience. I learned the most impressive lesson one morning on Cooper's Creek in the north Georgia mountains.

The Cooper's Creek flows through an isolated bit of rugged mountain wilderness between Lake Winfield Scott on the Wolfpen Gap road, and the valley where it levels out for a couple of miles and follows a more placid course through bottomland to join the Toccoa River.

Even though this last segment of the stream between the Suches-Margaret road and the river was the most heavily fished, Brad and I decided to try it. A hundred yards or so beyond the bridge, the creek washed through a deep pool that eddied against a rocky shoreline.

"This should hold a sizable rainbow," I commented. "Why don't you stay here and try it for a few minutes, and I'll fish on ahead. When you get through with this pool, walk downstream to where I am, then fish on ahead. In that way, we'll both get our share of virgin water."

Brad agreed and I left him at the pool, studying his box of flies for the right pattern.

I fished rather slowly—much slower than my normal pace—waiting for him to catch up, while I tried an assortment of dry and wet flies and nymphs in pools, eddies and riffles which seemed most likely to harbor a rainbow or brown. From time to time I looked over my shoulder, hoping to see my partner splashing downstream to join me. I snagged a couple of small rainbows—about eight or nine inches—and turned them back, but to save my soul could not seem to tie into a keeping-size trout that I knew should be on the prowl in this section of the creek.

By the time I reached the river, I was beginning to be a bit concerned about my partner. I glanced at my watch. I had been on the creek longer than two hours. I sampled a couple of pools in the Toccoa, then turned upstream, fishing as I went, but much faster than I had covered these waters before. I arrived at our starting pool more than three hours after I had left Brad there. I was relieved to find him standing in almost the same spot where I had last seen him. He was working a wet fly through the edge of the current against the far shore.

"You all right?" I asked.

"Sure. Why?"

"I was expecting you to follow me," I said. "There is some awfully good water between here and the river."

"This is pretty fair, too," he replied. "Did you do any good below here?"

"I raised only a couple of small ones," I admitted. "How about you?"

He showed me his creel. Packed in wet moss and ferns was a quartet of the loveliest rainbows, from twelve to fifteen inches. He had taken every one out of this very pool, while I was splashing my way to the river and back, and probably scaring the trout half out of their wits.

I have no idea how many good bucks I've missed simply because I did not have the patience to sit them out. I do know of one within the last few seasons.

Jack Crockford, Howard Verner and I were on a primitive weapons hunt in the Warwoman Wildlife Management Area in a mountainous corner of northeast Georgia. We were after bucks with our muzzle-loader rifles and had found abundant tracks and other sign to indicate that we should have every expectation of success.

Jack and I climbed a side of the mountain we had hunted the year before. About halfway up, where the trail forked, we paused a moment to blow and my partner made a suggestion.

"Why don't you go on straight to the top of the ridge. I'll swing to the right and hit the ridge lower down, so I can check for tracks around some of the white oak trees there. You wait for me on top and we'll make our plans for the remainder of the day."

I agreed and we separated. I climbed at a snail's pace, watching ahead for movement and taking time to look for sign. Where the trail forked again at the head of a small spring branch a couple of hundred yards from the top, several deer trails converged and the earth was cut to pieces with fresh tracks. I looked around for a few minutes, studying the lay of the land, then went on to our appointed meeting place on the crest.

From the tree I sat down by, I had a commanding view of the open woods on three sides and not a buck could have passed unnoticed within two hundred yards.

I manned the stand for a pair of hours, watching the lesser creatures of the woods move about me, but the longer I sat, the more convinced I became that the branch head where I had found so much sign was a better place than where I was parked at the moment. Jack was overdue at our rendezvous and I figured he must have found a likely spot and decided to wait it out for the remainder of the morning.

I got up and moved to the branch head, found a tree base from which I could see most of the small hollow, and put my carcass down for a long waiting period. No more than fifteen minutes passed before Jack came down the trail from the ridgetop. I whistled softly and he walked over to me.

"Did you see that big buck?"

"So far," I replied, "nothing more exciting than a squirrel has come this way."

He grinned.

"About a quarter of a mile down the ridge, I jumped a gosh-awful stag out of a thicket. The brush was too dense there to let me get a shot, but he headed up the ridge, so I just sat down and waited for you to shoot. When you didn't, I picked up the buck's tracks and trailed him right over the spot where you had been sitting."

"Don't mind me," I apologized. "That's the story of my life. I always move fifteen minutes or fifteen seconds too soon."

Sometimes I wonder just how much more game would be bagged if hunters exercised the same amount of patience as the animals themselves. A buck will stand dozens and more dozens of minutes, completely still until he interprets a sight or sound or smell. A squirrel will lie flattened out on a limb as long as you are in sight, or until it thinks danger has passed. With them it is a matter of survival and they take no chances. A hunter might possibly follow the same pattern if he knew that any movement he made would cost him his life.

Remaining in a state of immobility gives us an opportunity to exercise our other senses to the limits of their capabilities. You can hear other sounds better if you are not making some of your own. You can see movement more quickly when you are still. As you move through the woods, trees, bushes and other objects change location in relation to your eyes—those near you move more rapidly than the ones at the limit of your vision. This makes it appear that every object in the forest is shifting position, and when this is happening, the movements of animals, birds and other creatures are more difficult to see.

You cannot talk about patience without a discussion of turkey hunting, for this is perhaps the outdoor activity that requires more mental discipline than any other. I could write volumes on the gobblers I have missed by fractions of minutes because I did not have the patience to remain rooted in one spot quite long enough. One of those instances that stands out vividly in my memory happened on the Allison Lumber Company lands in western Alabama.

I was hunting there with Turkey Johnston, Jimmy Shirley and Bill Rae one spring when the gobblers appeared particularly cantankerous and unco-operative. We had hunted out the dawn hours with not one degree of success, had gone in for lunch and by mid-afternoon were on our way into a section of swamp where we had hopes of roosting a gobbler for the next morning's hunt.

Extending through the middle of this vast forested tract was a cleared area of perhaps sixty or seventy feet wide—I never found the time to measure it accurately—over a pipeline. The clearing was planted to grain for wildlife, and seeing deer or turkeys graze there at any time of day was not uncommon. Turkey and Jimmy were old hands at the game and never passed up an oppor-tunity to spot a gobbler wherever they thought they might see one. On any of the forest roads crossing the pipeline, they usually stopped the jeep and took a long look for a gobbler or a flock on or around the cleared strip. The pipeline was long and straight and they carried a pair of field glasses to help them iden-tify objects in the distance.

On this afternoon we spotted a pair of big gobblers about half a mile down the pipeline from the road. They stood for a moment while we looked them over, and when the jeep remained in one spot longer than the turkeys thought it should, they stepped out of sight into the woods.

"Let's try for them," Jimmy suggested.

"Suits me," Turkey agreed. "What do you propose?"

"There's a series of logging roads that will put us in line with the way they went," Jimmy said. "The four of us can scatter out through the woods, find a blind and call. One or both birds might come to investigate."

We followed his instructions and stationed ourselves about a hundred yards apart in a line that paralleled the pipeline clearing a quarter of a mile away. I found my spot in a myrtle thicket, built a blind by cutting short, heavily foliaged myrtle limbs and sticking them in a semicircle around me. I pulled on my camouflage mask to hide my face from my eyes down, arranged my body in a comfortable position, yelped a few times on my call and sat back to wait.

A turkey seldom gobbles after nine or ten o'clock in the morning, or until just before twilight, so waiting was about the only chance we had. Jimmy had suggested that we stick out the vigil until five o'clock and then move on to the roosting site.

I followed the rule of thumb of yelping every twenty minutes or so and straining my eyes and ears to the utmost in between times. I had been there longer than an hour when my ears picked up the low, inquiring note of a turkey. It was somewhere in front of me, but I could not determine how far. Very cautiously, I brought the gun to my shoulder, pointed in the general direction from which the yelp had come, and braced the gun into position with my elbows on my elevated knees.

I waited a long five minutes, then a much longer fifteen minutes, without seeing a movement or hearing another sound. The position of my gun, arms and knees became so burdensome that I lowered the gun to my lap for a few minutes.

You might guess that no more than sixty seconds later the gobbler's head appeared over the top of a small, thick bush no more than forty feet away and almost directly in line with the way my scattergun had been pointing. All I could see of the bird was from the eyes up, but the top of its head was broad and bright enough to tell me that I was looking at a big tom.

I could have killed him if only I had held my gun in position a minute longer. As it was, I was caught flatfooted with my shot pattern down. If I made a move to raise the gun, he would jerk his head down out of sight and be gone before I could pull the trigger. I had no choice but to wait for him to take a step away from that bush and then try to beat him to the draw.

As camouflaged as I was, he could only make out my outline, but knew that all was not copacetic around those premises. Even so, he stood there longer than I expected before he slowly pulled his head out of sight while I waited another five minutes for him to appear in another spot. When he clucked directly behind me, going away, I knew my chance was lost. Just one minute had reared its ugly head between success and failure.

Once, down at Brooks Holleman's Turkey Hollow in south Alabama, I waited most of the afternoon for a gobbler to show, then my patience ran out a split second too soon. I stood up in my blind to stretch my legs and a big tom which had stalked to within twenty yards of my yelper, and was just about to make its appearance, took to its wings and left me standing with my mouth open.

I hunted my prize turkey gobbler trophy for three years before I caught up with it. I really did not deserve it then, for my patience had long since run out, and except for an unusual set of circumstances, would have been long gone from the spot and never seen the bird.

My lack of nervous discipline came near licking me three different times on that particular day.

My wife, Kayte, and I, and an old outdoor partner, Phil Stone, had hunted out the hours between daylight and eight-thirty, in Tennessee's Ocoee Game Management Area, and just before mid-morning we met at the automobile parked on a mountain road. None of us had heard a turkey note all morning.

"Season's a bit late this year," Phil observed, "and it appears that these birds are not gobbling like they will when the weather warms up a bit."

"Kayte and I covered a big chunk of country back there and didn't hear a peep out of one," I agreed. "I'm ready to go to the cabin and sample that breakfast of country sausage and eggs."

We unloaded our guns, put them in the car, peeled off our camouflage outer garments, and I was ready to slide under the steering wheel when I had an inclination to make one more try. I pulled my gobbling box out of my hunting coat pocket, stepped to the edge of the road, gave the low notes of a hen and then made as raucous a gobble as the old box was capable of putting out.

I almost dropped my teeth when it was answered immediately from the next ridge, across a narrow cove. I knew the bird was an old one by the high pitch of his voice, and was almost certain that I could recognize that gobble I had been trying to catch up with for three seasons.

I put my finger against my lips to warn Kayte and Phil to silence, and while I was waiting for the tom to gobble again so I could tell which way he was traveling on the ridge, I slid into my hunting coat and camouflage netting and loaded the gun. When the bird gobbled again, he was almost a hundred yards down the ridge.

"You two stay here," I whispered. "I'm going to try to get in front of him, and I'll have to make a big circle and do some fast traveling."

I turned back under the crest of the divide flanked by the road and made a long detour to head the turkey, all the while giving myself a stiff lecture because we had come so close to going back to camp minutes too soon.

When I reached what I concluded was the right spot, I sat down and gave the low notes of a hen. Two gobblers answered this time—the first we had heard and a young tom off to the right.

The old tom arrived at a little gap that lay between us, then worked away from me through a creek valley and turned uphill toward the boundary of the management area, which was not yet open to hunting. I left the younger tom coming to my call and went after the old one, but by the time I reached the refuge boundary, he had already gone into the forbidden area.

I won't go into the excitement of the next two hours, most of which I spent pleading with the most dulcet hen notes I knew, or with ringing yelps and several lusty gobbles on my box.

The gobbler stood in one place on the mountain above me, sounding off periodically, and after that he shut up altogether.

Half an hour later I decided he had gone on deeper into the management area and that I'd have to wait until the season opened there. I hated to give up and sat for ten more minutes before I resigned myself completely to disappointment.

I had made up my mind to move and gather my things for the trip to the car when a stick cracked somewhere. Thinking it might be a deer, I strained to see the animal, but could make out no living thing in the woods ahead. For another ten minutes or more, I sat motionless and a second time was on the verge of giving up when I heard footsteps in the dry leaves. I would have bet my last powder grain that a man was walking toward me and possibly stalking my turkey call. Not especially enthusiastic about receiving a turkey load in either my face or backside, I froze to look and listen until I could be sure of the source of that sound.

That was when the big gobbler walked into view and stopped in a shaft of sunlight with his head high and the iridescent ripple of bronze, green, purple and gold that flowed over his body so resplendent that I caught my breath. I did not need a second look to tell me that he was the one. I had seen him so many times in the past three years that I would have recognized him walking down the street in front of my house.

I was also certain that this one gobbler would have lived a while longer had not luck or circumstances outweighed whatever patience I might have possessed.

Do not mistake the kind of patience we are talking about for meekness or submission, but rather an ability to adjust one's self to the passing of time, the ability to wait without fretting or building nervous tension simply by the waiting.

Some of my best action fishing pictures have been made after I sat for long hours with a camera in my hands and had begun to get itchy fingers for the feel of a rod. But I forced myself to hold to the camera for at least a while longer and was glad I had when my partner tied into a cavorting bass, trout or tarpon.

How does one without patience go about developing it? The easiest way must surely be by applying it to our everyday lives. This may involve a tremendous amount of that part of our character we know as self-control, especially if we have tendencies in the other direction.

I try to convince myself that I am expanding my supply of patience when I sit in a doctor's office awaiting my turn, or when I am standing in a long line with a basket of groceries to be checked out of the supermarket, or when I am waiting for someone who is late. Sometimes it takes a lot of guts to sit out a problem and do nothing about it until I have all the facts. I feel that these are the types of everyday training that add to our pleasure as well as to our success when we are in a duck or turkey blind, or holding down a deer stand where two well-padded game trails meet or cross.

One of our early philosophers pointed out that "genius is nothing else than a great aptitude for patience." The same might be said for successfully observing what goes on about you in the outdoors.

11 Your Senses Can Be Deceived

IF YOU HAVE spent enough time outdoors, you will know there are occasions and conditions under which your sense can hardly accept what your senses tell you, or when what you see or hear is not the way things are at all.

The most common example of this is the mirage.

The experts say that a mirage is "any number of different kinds of atmospheric optical illusions in which the observer sees non-existent bodies of water, oversize or inverted images of distant objects and various other distortions," and that it is formed when light is refracted as it passes through air having an unusual distribution of density.

More simply, most of us picture a mirage as a lake with all the trimmings, or a cool, green oasis, as seen by a thirsty wanderer in the desert. The water is usually a reflection of the sky and the oasis might be there, but a great distance away. But they prove that our eyes and other sense organs are capable of deceiving us.

Even a fish you watch in the water is an optical illusion. It is not at all where you see it. The reason is that when light waves traveling in one medium —in this instance, water—enter another medium of different density—the air— the velocity of the light is changed and it bends at an angle, making the fish or other underwater object appear farther away than it actually is.

Sound waves follow about the same pattern when they move through air of varying densities. The refraction of sound is said to be less apparent than that of light, but nonetheless, under the proper conditions, it is in evidence, and gives us what is known as an acoustic mirage. After a clear night without wind, we hear farther in early morning because the upward-moving rays of sound bend downward, and what we hear may be much more distant than we think.

The warmer the air, the faster sound waves travel, but hot or cold, they definitely are affected by the wind. We can hear a noise much farther when we are on the downwind side of it, and by the same token a crosswind may so affect sound waves that what we hear may seem in a different direction from where it really is. This is also true when a current of sound passes through two sharply divided layers of air with different densities. At this point it is capable of being refracted, in the same manner as light, and it is not our ears, but the sound effects themselves, that play tricks on us.

A third necessary ingredient which often works with sight and sound to deceive us is imagination. This is apportioned out in varying amounts to all humans, and most of us have enough so that often when we want to see or hear anything badly enough our senses make every effort to cooperate and make the thing we wish for come true.

SOUND ILLUSIONS

Water running over rocks has all the tones and inflections of the human voice, and several times when I was expecting to meet a couple of anglers on a trout stream I could hear them talking for hours before they finally showed up. What I had listened to was the lovely language of running water, and my imagination did not need much help to translate it into an exchange of words—however unintelligible—between my two partners.

Wind in a spruce or pine forest carries the same kind of sound effects, especially if you are expecting others to join you. Once in Montana I went to check on a forest fire where a crew was supposed to be at work. I heard them talking and laughing long before I got to the fire line and expected any minute to come in sight of the workers. The fire was dead out, but I walked completely around the fire line, which was a couple of miles long, hearing voices that I could never quite catch up with. I later learned that hours before I arrived the crew had completed its job and gone back to camp. What I had heard was the language of the wind as it moved through the spruce forest, but because I was expecting to find men there, my imagination gave me all the help it could.

If you are a turkey hunter, you will know that a score or more of voices in the woods so closely resemble the cluck or putt or yelp of a hen or the inquisitive "yowk" of a gobbler that you'd bet your last shell that it came from one of the big birds. Tree limbs caressing one another, the calls of crows and a dozen other birds will fool you, no matter how well acquainted you are with your quarry. A piliated woodpecker on a hollow stub in the distance can easily be mistaken for the ringing challenge of a gobbler.

A favorite trick of some hunters is to listen in a likely spot for turkeys to fly up to roost at dusk. With the birds located, they slip into the woods before daylight the next morning, stop close to the roost tree and call.

Late one afternoon in a south Georgia swamp, where I was trying to locate a roosting site, I heard several turkeys fly up into the trees within range of my ears but not my eyes. With me was a Yankee friend and I had him on the spot before daylight the next morning. I sat him in a blind and backed off into a clump of brush to call the birds past him.

Imagine my chagrin when a buzzard flew out of the tree where I thought the turkeys had gone to roost, and was followed by several more of the vultures, which came out one by one and sailed over us.

I was thankful to have enough brush between us so that my partner could not see me. I crawled away from the spot and made a circle through the swamp, hoping that while I was gone a real turkey would come to investigate the yelps I had made just before the buzzards flew over us. None did, and I never could quite bring myself to the point of telling my friend that I had roosted the wrong kind of birds.

OPTICAL ILLUSIONS

In turkey hunting your eyes as well as your ears often play tricks on you. The jagged projection of a small tree stump, an upright stick, a certain arrangement of leaves or limbs or rocks, may resemble one of the birds standing stock still with its head up. Once I called a gobbler up to the edge of an area choked with brush and small trees. I watched him walk within gun range and then lost him when he stepped behind a screen of leaves. I stared until my eyes bugged out and finally located him again, standing a few feet to one side of the leafy clump, behind which he had stepped only moments before. He stood stock still with his head up, and I could make him out very plainly, even through the heavy mass of brush.

I eased my gun up, drew a bead on his head, and when the gun roared the gobbler flew off. I knew I could not have missed at that range, so I walked over to see what had happened. Tracks in the soft earth showed that the big bird never got any farther than the leafy screen behind which he had disappeared. I wanted so desperately to see him that my eyes had created him out of a small tree that stood at just the right angle for a gobbler holding his head up, and my load of shot had given a good blistering to that tree.

I believe that many deer hunters are shot or shot at because some tyro gunner wants to see a buck so badly that anything that moves looks to him like a deer. I am thoroughly convinced that the two young hunters who took a shot at me identified me only as a trophy buck, even though I stood in plain, open view of them.

Earlier that morning on the same day, my wife, Kayte, and I had just missed being shot. We were sitting in a brushy clump at the base of a tree when four hunters came through the woods in such a manner that "tyro" was written all over them. They were stalking single-file, downwind, through leaves so noisy they could have been walking on cornflakes or potato chips. Each rifle barrel was pointed at the backside of the guy ahead. The foursome was angled to pass us by a hundred yards, so I whispered to Kayte, "Don't move and they'll go on by without seeing us."

Then the hunters changed direction and came up on a little knoll directly in front of us.

"Don't move," I whispered again.

Being a most obedient wife, she immediately put her hand up to rearrange her cap and one of the hunters saw the movement. He put his sights directly on her. I yelped and jumped to my feet, and even then he held his sights a few seconds longer before lowering his gun. I started toward the knoll and the quartet of hunters disappeared down the other side before I reached the top.

"I've had it," Kayte said. "Take me back to camp. I'll cook, wash dishes and make the beds. If you want venison, you'll have to bring it in on your own."

It was not my day. That afternoon I climbed into a mountain gap where two game trails crossed—one along the ridge and the other crossing between wide, flat hollows on each side of the mountain.

I sat with my back to a large tree where I could watch both trails. The forest around me was the open hardwood type with excellent visibility for a hundred and fifty yards.

I had been there an hour when two hunters came down the ridge trail. They appeared to be in their late 'teens. They stopped about fifty yards from where I sat and held a whispered conversation. Remembering how the hunter at daylight that morning had suddenly "discovered" Kayte and me and put his sights on us, I considered it might be wise to make my presence known. The two boys were facing almost in my direction, so I simply got to my feet and waved my hand at them.

They stood for a fraction of a second as though they could not believe their eyes, then one of them excitedly jabbed a finger several times in my direction. The other threw up his rifle and I found myself looking right down the gun barrel. I threw up my hand again and yelled, "Hey!" and when he didn't lower the gun in a fraction of a second, I dived behind the base of the tree. I wasn't a bit too soon, either. The gun went off just as I hit the ground.

I raised my head, peeped cautiously around the tree and saw that he was no longer pointing the rifle in my direction. I got to my feet and stepped out from behind the tree trunk, rifle in my hand, and started toward the boys, who turned immediately to retreat up the trail.

"Wait a minute," I called.

They kept walking.

"If you don't stop," I said, "I'll kill both of you."

They stopped then and when I got close enough, I could see the terror of what they had almost done in their eyes.

"What the hell did you think you were shooting at?" I demanded.

With his hand shaking, one of the boys pointed downhill.

"At—that—that hollow—tree," he stammered.

"Did you expect a deer to run out of the hollow?" I asked. I said a few more things too, and there's no need to repeat them here, but the more I thought about it, the more convinced I was that those kids were so anxious to carry home a deer, that even standing tall and two-legged, I looked like one to them.

When he didn't lower the gun in a fraction of a second, I dived behind the base of the tree.

Illusion in the outdoors may be more common with less experienced persons, but they do not have a monopoly on it. A seasoned woodsman will sometimes be misled by what he thinks he sees.

One of my top guides and hunting partners in western Wyoming over the years was Frank Lasater. He knew the business of hunting western big game from the inside out and taught me a great deal about his country and the game animals there. He was the sort of fellow you like to have around when the going gets rough, and he was a right handy guy to have aboard when all was fine and dandy, too.

I had bagged my elk—an oversized six-point bull. We spent a day or two after that in productive cutthroat trout waters, and then decided to go looking for a mule deer with big feet. We had seen its tracks on one of the high ridges up the Thorofare from Hammett Cabin.

Frank and I tied our horses and spent most of the day pussyfooting around the ridgetop, looking into the draws, glassing the bases of cliffs where we might find a buck lying out of the wind, hunting hard and seriously and enjoying every minute of it.

Late in the afternoon we were on our way to where we had left the horses and my eye caught a flicker of movement in a thicket ahead. I stopped so suddenly that Frank, walking behind, collided with my rear bumper. I fumbled for my binoculars, focused them on the spot where I had seen the movement and made out the outline of a deer, standing motionless.

"It's that big buck," I whispered. "I never saw such a rack."

Frank put his glasses on the animal and whistled under his breath.

"Look at the beams on those antlers," he said. "If that ain't a record head, I never saw one."

All this time I was slowly sliding the gunsling off my shoulder, trying to be as easy as possible and not startle the deer. I put the crosshairs in my scope on a spot behind the front shoulder, pushed the safety off and took the slack out of the trigger.

I have no idea what delayed the shot. It must have been that sixth sense, but I did hesitate just long enough for the mulie to take a step forward. He moved, but his antlers didn't. I was so dumbfounded that it's a wonder I did not squeeze down on the trigger anyway.

The doe was large enough to be a buck, and after she moved on, Frank and I spent another ten minutes studying that arrangement of tree branches under which the animal had stood, and marveling that it could so closely resemble a set of antlers. We moved toward it then, and the closer we got, the more those tree limbs began to look like limbs. But from where we had first spotted them, I am afraid I would have had an illegal doe on my hands if she had not moved at just the right moment.

FATIGUE AND THE SENSES

I have found that one of the conditions that helps to inspire imagination is fatigue. When you are tired, your ears and eyes do not work as well, and you are much more likely to be victimized by illusion. I was on my way into camp one night with a fellow who did not have much experience at big game hunting. We had been on the trail before daylight and were so weary that our eyeballs sagged.

Half a mile or so below camp, we rode in that period of daylight when the stars begin to appear and the light is almost gone in the forest. We were plodding along through a little park when my companion suddenly reined in his horse, jumped out of the saddle and dragged his rifle from its scabbard.

"What is it?" I asked.

"A moose," he hissed, "and a big one."

He pumped a shell into his chamber, threw up the gun, and then I saw that he was focused on a dark chestnut horse in a far corner of the clearing.

"No! No!" I fairly yelled.

I hit the ground and was beside him in two jumps.

"You're about to gun down one of the outfitter's saddle horses."

I finally prevailed on him to ride closer for a better look, and he could not believe his eyes. We had been hunting for a good moose, and he was so worn

The deer took a step forward, but his "antlers" didn't move.

out from the long day that when that horse moved, to him it could not have been anything but a moose.

There must be a moral here somewhere, about never pulling that trigger until you are unquestionably sure of what is in line with those sights.

For years I have preached that fatigue is one of the gravest dangers in the woods, fields and on the waters. In addition to creating illusions such as my hunting partner had, it tends to make a man careless when he is out of doors and carelessness can be a crippler or a killer.

The mind is never at its best when muscles are exhausted and body juices at low ebb. And when the mind is tired, nerves and muscles do not react so quickly. Some of my closest calls in the woods have come near the end of long, tough days in the saddle or afoot on rooftop mountains.

Years ago I'd go skipping over any type of terrain and never give it a second thought. But many seasons of experience and bruises have taught me to move much slower and more carefully, testing every rock and log for firmness before I put my full weight on it, picking the easiest route around obstacles, and so on. I now try to be as deliberate in all of my outdoor activities as I expect to be when and if I ever become a nonagenarian.

From the lips of hunters, some of whom were old-timers, I've heard of too many painful hours spent crawling out to a trail or road because of broken legs or other broken bones. These accounts are no more attractive than the stories of frozen, foodless days during which a fellow was barely able to drag himself around enough to gather twigs and limbs for an inadequate campfire until he was found.

By rather direct and indiscreet inquiry, I have learned that most of the accidents that get hunters into such tight spots result from carelessness caused by fatigue.

In the Cascade Range of Washington state, I spent many hunting days afoot around Blizzard Peak. This exceptionally rugged mountain has slides of unstable rocks and slopes so angled that they are often difficult to navigate. When the weather is warm, as it was then, those are the spots most likely to produce a big buck.

Most of my clambering around the big peak was on my own. Being in strange country, I followed the usual routine of moving slowly and carefully. But the high altitude and exertion made me weary and I began to let down my barrier of caution. I didn't realize this until it was almost too late.

After spending a most unsuccessful morning on the high ridges, I decided to go into camp, only two or three miles down the mountain, for lunch and a short siesta.

The steep slope was dotted with stubby fir trees and I found that by holding onto one low tree after another, I could keep my footing easier and make better time downhill. But because I was tired, I got impatient and careless and began to swing from tree to tree down the slope, a lot like a monkey making time through the jungle.

It had to happen—every circumstance was right. On one especially angled ridge, my boot hit a loose rock which turned over under my foot. The top of the last tree tore from my hand. I was traveling so fast that my momentum carried me into the air, over a ten-foot ledge.

It was nothing but good fortune that the slope at the foot of the ledge was soft earth and not one of those treacherous rock slides. I landed on my back, atop the rifle that was slung over my shoulder, and skidded another ten feet downhill.

After the stars quit popping through my head, I sat up. All of my parts seemed to be in working order except my right arm. I couldn't lift it and for a moment was sure it had been broken. As it turned out, I had only temporarily paralyzed a muscle in the shoulder that landed on the rifle, but it gave me a bad time for the remainder of the trip. I could blame the accident only on carelessness brought on by my fatigue.

One of the hazards I must constantly watch for in the woods is the jagged end of a snag or broken limb about face high. Several times I have literally run into such protruding limbs. The last one might have cost me an eye.

We were following cougar dogs up a mountain on Vancouver Island in British Columbia. Some of the mountain sheep country I've seen wasn't half so steep, and my knees were making a tremendous effort to keep my shanks and thighs from falling apart.

My head was down. When I raised it to see what course the guide had taken around the rock cliff above us, one side of my face struck the sharp end of a broken limb. The blow was so close to my eye that it knocked my glasses off. The rims deflected the stick, but it cut a gash like an ax wound into my cheek.

This injury, caused basically by fatigue, was bloody, painful and inconvenient. It could have been much more serious.

I have experienced the same buildup of weariness on a rough trout stream. I start out the day fresh, confident of my footing on underwater rocks, bouncing from one boulder to another like a mountain goat. As the day wears on, however, my footing becomes less sure. I am more likely to step on a loose or slippery stone than to step over it. I lose some of my sense of balance. I don't feel tired or less enthusiastic—each new pool holds the same charm and challenge as the last.

But when I recognize those symptoms of fatigue—impatience and carelessness—I heed them by resting a while in the shade or even by leaving the stream entirely. Few trout are worth a broken leg or cracked noggin.

One could write at great length about this and the other odd and out-of-the-ordinary circumstances any outdoorsman will encounter if he spends many days in the mountains or swamps or wherever, but it is all a part of that wonderful world out there, in which the proper use of both your sense and senses will make each hour a safe, delightful and refreshing one.

12 The Rewards

THERE MUST have been a time somewhere in man's habitation of this earth when every move he made, everywhere he went and everything he did was governed by Nature's first law of survival. He was either hunting for food, escaping danger or satisfying needs on which depended either his own existence or the perpetuation of his race.

To some extent we, as moderns, continue to observe the basic rules of survival, but under different circumstances. We no longer have to scratch like a bear in decaying logs for grubs, or dig for tubers, or search the forest for fruits, nuts and berries in season, or stalk our meat with a rock or club. A large percentage of the world's population today is literally and figuratively "out of the woods." We live in comfortable houses with heat and light and water piped in from outside sources. For the majority of us urban dwellers, food comes in loaves, cans, boxes, jars, sacks and frozen or unfrozen packets—all prepared commercially. In season we supplement this with some fresh food if we own a garden, or know someone who does.

To get enough to eat and remain comfortable, all we need is money for such things as rent, food, utilities, clothes, entertainment and taxes, and we get this by selling our time in one way or another. For many of us, this means indoor jobs which take up most of our hours when we are awake. To these efforts we often apply such facetious terms as "the old salt mine," "the daily grind," and "keeping our noses to the grindstone."

In one sense we have "arrived." A few thousands of generations ago, man set out to be exactly where he is today, congregated in communities for protection and companionship, with a guaranteed source of subsistence with little physical effort.

In another sense, we have walked toward the sun for hundreds of thousands of years without ever getting far from the jungle. Now that we have reached our present pinnacle of "civilization"—if one may so loosely use a word—something impels us and we are gradually swinging back the other way. Not only in America, but in nations all over the world where living standards are high, people are moving outdoors, not necessarily to make a livelihood there, but to satisfy some inherent urge that belongs to the ages.

We leave the comforts of home to sleep on the ground, warm beside campfires of our own making, and put ourselves through unnecessary hardships—for what reason? We may claim that when we hunt or fish, we are after meat. This is our excuse for being there, but we are searching for something that goes much deeper than belly demands that we can more easily satisfy at the corner grocery store.

Our deep-seated need is to prove that we are still capable of providing for ourselves with a minimum of outside assistance. In the ranks there may be some who kill for the sheer lust of killing, but these are in the negligible minority. The vast pleasure most of us get is in the operation to the utmost of our outdoor sense and senses. One evidence of this is the growing number of sportsmen who are putting aside the modern, highly efficient high-powered rifle to hunt with the older muzzle-loader and the much older bow and arrow. These fellows are not after meat as much as they are the pleasure of the hunt and the satisfaction of accomplishment.

This same quality applies to the non-hunter as well. Why will a man put a pack on his back and spend two weeks walking along the crest of a mountain through wilderness country, from one paved highway to another, when he could make the journey between the same two points by automobile in a few hours? What he is searching for is primitive adventure, hardships to toughen his muscles and his mind, escape into a world where his ability to see, hear, feel and exercise his basic judgment makes him feel that he is touching fingers with the past.

The tangible reward that any person finds in the outdoors depends on that particular individual, and on his reason for being there. With one man it may be a big-game trophy to hang on his den wall, and with another a lunker trout he has been trying to entice with a fly. A photographer's prize catch is a striking picture. A student of birds is repaid many times over for his patience when he records a species new to him, or is able to jot down an especially early arrival date for one of the migrants. A hiker reaps the benefits of exercise and of fresh air in his lungs, and for the nature lover, the reward may be the discovery of a flower, or mushroom, or butterfly he is able to identify.

The extent of these rewards is dependent on how well we have developed our powers of observation and are able to use our basic senses.

The more one is aware of the drama and comedy in the wilderness world through which he moves, the surer he is that the least important moment of a hunt is the one in which he pulls the trigger, and that the success of a fishing trip does not depend on the size and number of the fish. The outdoorsman often lives through and remembers other portions of his experience long after he has forgotten the "moment of truth," as one storyteller tagged what he considered to be the climax of his hunt.

Not long ago the editor of a state game and fish publication asked me to do a short article for him on hunting and fishing. I feel that what I wrote for him, in a way expresses the changing philosophy of almost everyone who today devotes himself in one way or another to the outdoors and the many pleasures he harvests there through all of his senses, however dull or bright, or trained or untrained they might be. Here is what I said:

Somewhere ahead we heard the thunder of a waterfall. It filled the canyon with overtones that was background music to the symphony of the riffles under our feet. We passed up a likely pool and splashed ahead to a sweeping bend of the river and stood in awe at the spectacle before us.

The river left its canyon bed on the mountainside and leapt into space, its solid volume of water disintegrating, as it fell, into distorted columns of spray. The slanting sun made it look like a shower of silver, set in the emerald of laurel banks and hemlock trees, with its base a turquoise pool carved in massive boulders.

"This is yours," my stream partner announced cheerfully. "I fished the last one."

"You go ahead," I murmured. "I'll sit this one out."

He slid into the water and became a part of the tableau, the end of his nylon line flicking at the hidden corners of the pool. Suddenly the rod leapt in his hands and seemed to become a living part of him. The largest rainbow we had seen that day erupted from the depths of a rocky cavern, throwing its body through such an aerial performance that I thought of poetry in slow motion.

My partner played his catch skillfully through three more jumps, held a taut line while his rainbow bored for safety in the depths, and finally brought his fish on its side and within reach of his net. He splashed back to where I sat, his face lit up like a neon bass bug, and held up the twenty-incher for me to see.

"That is a beauty," I agreed.

He lowered the fish and regarded me suspiciously.

"That was really your pool. Why didn't you want to fish it?"

"I wouldn't have had it any other way," I assured him. "What I'll remember here is more enduring than any trout."

"Why do you fish at all?" he demanded.

I shrugged and relit my pipe. If he did not understand by then, he never would.

"Let's detour around this hunk of granite and find another hole," I suggested. "You've done right well by this one."

As we climbed our mountain stream that day, I continued to ponder my partner's question. Why, indeed, did I fish—and hunt? Why does anyone? Obviously, that question could get a hundred different answers. Maybe more. And each would be in keeping with the character of the individual giving the answer.

No one knows for sure, but reducing animals, birds, fish and other creatures to the substance meals are made of must have originated out of hunger. Man is, and has always been, a predator; that is, he preyed on the creatures around him—and no doubt some of them preyed on him—to get his daily vittles.

Over the millenniums we have constantly improved our techniques for taking game and fish—from club to spear and arrow and gorge to the modern high-powered rifle and artfully designed fishing gear.

In spite of these changes, there remains in most of us the urge and instinct to single-handedly venture forth and bring home the makings of a family meal. To know that we can accomplish this gives us a feeling of security—and its actual accomplishment gives us a sense of satisfaction and importance.

Basically—under the veneer of civilization we have acquired over a few million years—this is probably the reason man finds so much gratification in the arts of hunting and fishing.

But there are other reasons which, in the complexities of modern existence, are every bit as important as the satisfaction of those instincts brought down from the cave days. Most of us do lead a highly complicated existence, revolving around profit and loss, taxes, wars, elections, mechanical gadgets and any number of other modern frustrations which constantly tear at our emotions. To help combat physical, mental and moral fatigue caused by the daily pressure, business wisely provides a certain amount of time each year for relaxation. We call it a vacation and this change of activity—even for a short period—is necessary to keep most of us from ending up in the bughouse.

In a sense every hunting trip, every fishing trip, and every excursion into the outdoors—no matter what the purpose or the duration—is an escape from those complexities which surround us. Our motivating influence may be to satisfy that age-old urge to put meat on the table—but the other rewards are much more lasting than a mouthful of meat.

Like my fishing partner and me at the waterfall—to save my soul I could never tell you what became of that trout: the memory of the beauty and the music of the moment is one of the bright spots of my outdoor year.

What are those things you are most likely to recall when you sit down and think of the last time you were in the woods, or on a lake or stream?

I remember a campfire in the cold, black heart of the night. Its flames threw ragged shadows behind the trees, its shower of sparks died on the wings of the darkness. We broiled a steak over it on a two-pronged hickory spit cut out of the woods—the aroma of coffee came from an old pot set on coals raked out of the golden heart of the fire. The flames crackled and spat and whispered and sang to keep up a cheerful conversation while it drove back the barriers of the night and embraced us in the aura of its warmth. You can get more heat out of a stove or furnace, but not the friendship you feel with your campfire on an autumn night.

I remember the corner of a lake at sundown. The wind had died, the surface was mirror-still. At the end of the cove a wood thrush played its solemn flute and a squirrel barked from the hillside. The sun had gone, but it left vermilion clouds splayed across the sky, and as these began to fade, a bass splashed against the shoreline. We laid a frog popper in the middle of the wake left by the largemouth, let the ripples die, and worked it out with a gurgling sound that added to the soft music of sundown. A real frog grunted from the bank behind us, and peepers scattered along the shoreline took up the chorus. The bass we tried to entice ignored our offerings, but that was all right. The dying day was sufficient unto itself.

I remember perching in a mesquite tree on the Texas-Mexican border. A mesquite has thorns in the most unexpected places. Its limbs are brittle and you don't dare quite trust one to support your weight. So I distributed my body as best I could on several of the branches, held on to my rifle and kept an eye peeled on a well-used deer trail that ran under the tree. A huge hawk lit in the topmost branches and peered down at me. A group of javelinas came by, grunting at one another and probing in the soft dirt for what kind of food I had no idea. A dog coyote trotted by, came to my trail, sniffed at it and paused to study the terrain ahead before moving on. I did not see the buck I was after, and did not care especially for sitting long hours in a mesquite tree, but would not have missed that afternoon for any price.

I remember an arctic afternoon, when the red mark on the thermometer stood at almost half a hundred degrees below zero. Now and then a tree limb popped and I knew that its juices had frozen under the intense cold. The snow was halfway to my knees and made a muffled tinkle when I moved. Moose trails showed in the snow and the trail of a snowshoe rabbit—the hare that turns from brown to white when the snow flies—crossed the moose tracks. The air was so cold it felt hot to my lungs, and in spite of heavy clothes and wool and horsehide mittens, I had to keep moving to save myself from congealing completely. Who could ever forget such an afternoon in a barren, white wasteland of mid-winter?

I've taken game and fish—sure—but the kills and catches are not what I remember most about the outdoors. As important as the memories I bring home are the things I leave in the woods and fields and on the waters. They are the dumping ground for my tension and worry and nerves worn thin by the friction of what we call civilization. I breathe the polluted air out of my lungs and wash my face and hands clean of the grime. I get the jangle of the telephone, radio, television, jukebox, the blare of horns and scream of motors out of my ears.

I find peacefulness and solitude, and music not of the trumpet or drum. I am refreshed and invigorated, and I remember to look up into the hills and give thanks that there are still a few spots where one can go to get away from it all.

Bibliography

Bauer, Erwin. *Outdoor Photography.* New York: Popular Science Publishing Company, 1965.

Brasher, Rex. *Birds and Trees of North America.* New York: Columbia University Press, 1968.

Breland, Osmond P. *Animal Life and Lore.* New York: Harper & Row Publishers, 1964.

Burt, William H. & Grossenheider, R. P. *Field Guide to the Mammals.* Boston: Houghton Mifflin Company, 1964.

Colby, Carroll B. *Fish & Wildlife.* New York: Coward-McCann, Inc., 1955.

Collins, Henry H. *Complete Field Guide to American Wildlife: East, Central & North.* New York: Harper & Row Publishers, 1959.

Dalrymple, Byron. *Sportsman's Guide to Game Fish.* New York: Outdoor Life Books, Popular Science Publishing Company, Inc., 1968.

Dolan, Ellen M. & Kestleloot, E. *Animals in Their Homes: Aquatic Dwellings.* New York: McGraw-Hill Book Company, 1967.

Fenton, C. L. & Pallas, Dorothy C. *Birds and Their World.* New York: John Day Company, Inc., 1954.

Hanford, Barbara. *Animals In Their Homes: Nests.* New York: McGraw-Hill Book Company, 1967.

Kine, Russ. *Complete Book of Nature Photography.* New York: American Book Company, 1962.

Mason, George F. *Animal Tracks.* New York: William Morrow & Company, Inc., 1943.

Mellanby, H. *Animal Life in Freshwater.* New York: Barnes & Noble, Inc., 1963.

Morgan, Ann. *Field Book of Animals in Winter.* New York: G. P. Putnam's Sons, 1939.

Murie, Olaus. *Field Guide to Animal Tracks.* Boston: Houghton Mifflin Company, 1954.

Ormond, Clyde. *Complete Book of Outdoor Lore.* New York: Harper & Row Publishers, 1965.

Parmeley, J. *Animals in Their Homes: Burrows & Apartments.* New York: McGraw Hill Book Company, 1967.

Peterson, Roger T. *Bird Watcher's Anthology.* New York: Harcourt, Brace & World, 1957.

Peterson, Roger T. *Birds Over America.* New York: Dodd, Mead & Company, 1964.

Peterson, Roger T. *Field Guide to the Birds.* Boston: Houghton Mifflin Company, 1947.

Peterson, Roger T. & Fisher, James. *Wild America.* Boston: Houghton Mifflin Company, 1955.

Peterson, Roger T. *Wildlife in Color.* Boston: Houghton Mifflin Company, 1951.

Stoutenburg, Adrien. *Animals At Bay: Rare & Rescued American Wildlife.* New York: Doubleday & Company, Inc., 1968.

Reed, Chester A. *Bird Guide: Land Birds East of the Rockies.* New York: Doubleday & Company, Inc., 1964.

Robbins, Chandler et al. *Birds of North America: A Guide to Field Identification.* New York: Golden Press, 1968.

Rue, Leonard Lee. *Sportsman's Guide to Game Animals.* New York: Outdoor Life Books, Popular Science Publishing Company, Inc., 1968.

Seton, Ernest T. *Animal Tracks & Hunter Signs.* New York: Doubleday & Company, Inc., 1958.

INDEX

INDEX

Acoustic mirage, from refraction of sound, 92–93
Action fishing pictures, and exercise of patience in taking of, 91
Angler's eye, *see* Fisherman's eye
Animal sounds, and messages conveyed, 64–72
 of animals cataloged as "wild," 64–65
 bird talk, 65–67
 developing a sensitive ear for, 70–72
 use of tape recorder in, 71–72
 of familiar domesticated pets, 64
 of squirrels, 67–68, 71
Antelope, eyesight of, 6
Anvil bone of ear, 57–58
Atlanta *Journal and Constitution,* Kenneth Rogers as photographer for, 43
Auditory nerve fibres, 58

Bait fish splashing on surface, as indication of presence of game fish, 29
Bait fishing, 29
Barfish, *see* White bass fishing
Basilar membrane of ear, 58
Bass fishing:

 in Florida's freshwater lakes and rivers, 29
 see also White bass fishing
Bear, different sounds of, conveying different messages, 64–65
Bear hunting in Alaska, and misreading of age of bear tracks, 49
Big-game hunting:
 in Canadian Rockies, and faulty judging of distance, 44–45
 scouting in advance of season for tracks and sign, 47
 use of binoculars in, 41–43
Big-game trophies, 102
Binoculars:
 focusing arrangement of, 42
 increase in enjoyment of outdoors from use of, 43
 methods of carrying on hunting trips, 42–43
 price of, 41
 specifications for a "good" glass for bird study or hunting, factors to be considered in, 41–42
 use of, by bird students and hunters of big-game animals, 41–43
 use of, by fishermen, to spot circling sea birds, 29
Bird feeders, 40